My
Mother's
Daughter

ALSO EDITED BY IRENE ZAHAVA

Anthologies
Finding Courage
Hear the Silence
Lesbian Love Stories
Lesbian Love Stories: Volume Two
Love, Struggle and Change
My Father's Daughter
Speaking for Ourselves
Through Other Eyes
Word of Mouth

The WomanSleuth Mystery Series
The WomanSleuth Anthology
The Second WomanSleuth Anthology
The Third WomanSleuth Anthology

Journals
Earth Songs
Moonflower
Water Spirit

My Mother's Daughter

Stories by Women

EDITED BY IRENE ZAHAVA

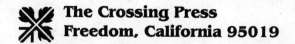 **The Crossing Press**
Freedom, California 95019

Dedicated to my mother,
Eve Levinson

Library of Congress Cataloging-in-Publication Data

My mother's daughter : stories by women / edited by Irene Zahava.
    p. cm.
   ISBN 0-89594-465-0   ISBN 0-89594-464-2 (pbk.)
    1. Mothers and daughters--United States--Fiction. 2. Short stories,
American--Women authors. 3. Women--United States--Fiction.
I. Zahava, Irene.
PS648.M59M9   1991
813'.01089287--dc20   90-28898
                        CIP

Contents

Preface

My mother was twenty-three years old when she gave birth to me. Over the past forty years she has taught me many lessons:

Nothing is as it appears.

There are no calories in a broken cookie.

When in doubt, throw it out.

A stuffed animal is easier to care for than a baby.

You can never own too many pairs of shoes.

Once you start a container of ice cream you may as well finish it.

If you wear shoulder pads under a T-shirt you'll be appropriately dressed for almost every occasion.

Never trust anyone with a secret — except your mother.

More and more often I open my mouth and my mother's words come out. I've started to hold my hands and gesture the way she does, and I'm told that I now laugh with her laugh. Unfortunately, the old saying that a woman grows up to become her mother is not usually meant as a compliment, but I hope to be so lucky.

Irene Zahava

Mother

MARILYN KRYSL

In the beginning there was my mother. A shape. A shape and a force, standing in the light. You could see her energy; it was visible in the air. Against any background she stood out. Heat radiating from her blurred objects as she moved past them so that it seemed her skin gave off a charge. Even sitting, writing a letter, sewing, or drinking a cup of coffee, she was kinetic, animated. They could have used her instead of Ready Kilowatt to see electricity. A buffer of radiance surrounded her, she gave off light.

My father was gone to the war. I was two and three and four, but I remembered him, checked my memory against the photograph on my mother's dressing table. A handsome man, though distant in the gilded frame, like the photograph of Clark Gable my mother kept on the other side. Two movie stars, from a realm not beyond but away, someplace I'd heard about but never seen, Tokyo, Guam, Hollywood, San Juan

Capistrano. My father was not there to take me on the Tiltawhirl or teach me to tie my laces.

My mother worked as the manager of Kovacs' Drycleaning, and I was allowed to go with her and play while she manned the shop and ran the presser. I played hide-and-seek with myself among the racks of pressed suits, smoothed my cheeks against the skirts of rayon dresses. When I was tired I climbed onto the shelf below the cash register and curled up with my blanket. From there I could see my mother lift the presser arm, adjust the shirt, bring the arm precisely down. Again and again she repeated this series of movements, absolutely perfectly timed. Her graceful precision pleased me immensely, and I lay on the shelf watching her until heat and drowsiness overwhelmed me and I fell asleep.

Kovacs didn't mind me being there because Mama was industrious. He had probably never before had anyone quite so good at running his business. Because he was making money, my presence could be overlooked. He would come in to check on things, and invariably things were buzzing. Water surged in tubs, masses of wet clothes churned in vats of starch, irons, and spot-remover hoses hissed, the presser clanked and belched steam. It was my mother who made these things happen. He puffed on thick cigars and was satisfied.

Life, I thought, was busy, productive. We were workers, the world was a place where people made things, did things. And it was this making and doing that made the world go. When my mother pressed shirts, swept linoleum, washed windows or brushed her hair, she seemed substantial, some-one to be reckoned with. She made clothes clean, windows bright, and floors smooth. Produce flourished in her wake, flowers spread across earth beds. As we walked home from Kovacs' in the early evening she made pickups roll by, and a tractor at the edge of town pull a harrow through black ground. I heard far off the kiss of milk against the sides of pails, the soft thud of hens' eggs settling into nests. Because of her the grain elevator filled, we would have bread. The smell of bread rising, the sound of the treadle sewing machine, these were her talismans.

What I wanted was to be where she was. Where she was the current was faster, the light more brilliant, the colors brighter. Air turned stale when she was gone, scintillant when she was there. She enhanced the ordinary present with her presence, made the quotidian more interesting than otherwise. I felt not that something was about to happen, but that something was happening now. I learned the reverberations of moment heaped upon moment. A word was important because she had spoken it, the vibrations of her voice continued to energize the local air indefinitely. A chunk of granite flecked with mica became a sacred stone because she picked it up, put it down. When she left a room, the space kept a faint residue of her presence. Nothing alive and touched by her hand could ever again be simply dull, dead matter.

She left dishes undone to help me perfect handstands, wrestling and giggling with me, tumbling me against her. She was lavish with hugs, making a big to-do lifting me to her lap, urging me closer, settling me against her. She read stories, taught me cat's cradle and witch's broom, laughed prettily at my remarks. She talked the butcher into giving her sheets of butcher paper for my drawings. And she got down on the floor on her hands and knees and admired the accumulating crayon, urging me on to grander sweeps all the way across that great, open field.

When I looked at pictures of families in magazines, it didn't occur to me to imagine myself grown, with a husband and child of my own. These pictures referred only to us, now: I was the child, she was the mother, this was a fact that would not change. I expected to spend my life with her, and at the very least I wanted her to notice me, recognize the intensity of my passion. I blazed with fidelity. For the opportunity to perform some act of service I could endure inconvenience, discomfort, insult. I rushed to open screen doors, car doors, church doors for her. I brought her hourly offerings — nosegays, the best weeds, rocks, and feathers. I would bring her necklace from the dressing table, borrow cups of sugar, mail letters in any weather. I even went out alone in the dark to roll up the windows of the Chevy.

I was a kind of miniature, inept attendant, an awkward, dwarf lady-in-waiting. I'd go anywhere at all, wait any length of time. I waited with snow melting inside my galoshes, my mittens wet and beginning to freeze. I waited with an empty stomach, a dry mouth, a full bladder. In heat or cold, waiting to pay the water bill, standing on the sidewalk amid the din of gossip, I nestled against her haunch, clung to her dress or the sleeve of her muskrat jacket. And when I couldn't stand up any longer, I sat down cross-legged on floor or sidewalk and looked up at her.

Sometimes I hoped she would be a little sick so I could bring her boxes of Kleenex, aspirin, cups of soup. But if there were no errands, no arduous tasks, no extra gratification I could bring to her, then waiting was itself a busy activity, using up calories, leaving me worn out but with a sense of accomplishment. I was the kind of slave every despot dreams of, moral judgment suspended, burning to do service.

When I began to get the idea that she wanted more than we had, that she hoped to escape Kovacs' for something bigger, I was disappointed. I had thought it was work itself, that marvelous motion, that was the point. It had looked that way to me when I looked at her: *let me be in motion like her*. And if I came to her whining I had nothing to do, my mother was indignant. "The world is filled with things to do," she would say. "Build cities, tame rivers. Take out the trash."

But for my mother Kovacs' wasn't paradise. This marvelous enterprise was something dimmer, less divine than I'd thought. She had begun to talk about cities, to incant the names of distant places. San Diego, Los Angeles, Monterey. San Francisco, Portland, Seattle. When she said these names her eyes looked away from mine, looked above me into the distance. She threw herself into work at Kovacs' like she was throwing something noxious away.

The more dissatisfied she became, the harder she worked. We started going to Kovacs' earlier, staying later. When I watched her now, hurrying, a drop of perspiration at her temple, I saw this motion beginning to wear her away, grain by grain. It was as though at Kovacs' she was locked in combat with some force she had to best.

"Hurry," she said. "You have to take a bath, quick." She stood beneath the door's arch, her shoulders vulnerable, nightgown just touching the floor. "Hurry, please." Behind her the early light, dim gold. I heard the first bird, a dove.

I slid out of bed, followed her down the hall. While the tub filled she pulled the nightgown over her head, stood at the sink, and turned on both faucets. Her breasts hung soft and loose, the hair of her crotch tight curls, blond with a reddish tinge. She washed her face, her throat, her shoulders quickly, oblivious to light, the music of the water. Hurrying, she dried herself. Her mind raced ahead, to Kovacs', to business.

The hairless fold between my legs was dampsoft, I put my hand down there to feel my oils. I liked the smell, the taste on my fingers; I would undo the bodice between my thighs, like I pulled the laces from my shoes. The dove cooed softly. I began to hum. Then my mother turned to me. *Not now,* her look told me. *We're in a hurry. Some other time, not now.* And she lifted me into the tub, soaped a washcloth, scrubbed me hard, as though pressure were speed. Rinsed me fast, lifted me out. With a towel she smothered my nakedness, closed the million pores of my skin.

She left me then, walked briskly back to her bedroom.

5

The light had lost its gold flush. The dove, silent. What I heard was water draining from the tub. A sad sound, water leaking slowly down a hole.

Still I adored her. Or I had determined to adore her, no matter what: I did not want paradise with qualifications. I wanted paradise pure. If it was not quite so, still I might pretend it was. August, the county fair, my mother's hand in mine. "Please," I said, "can we look at the pigs?"

We walked through dusk to the livestock barn, under the wide doorway draped with bunting. The roof vaulted over low pens, muddy aisles. A din of snores, cacophony of squeals. I had seen pigs, fed my grandparents' sow and piglets, but I'd failed to notice the phenomenon of pigs: so there was crudity on the graceful earth. Who, I wondered, was responsible for hog and sow, waddling fatsacks, coarse skin stuck with wiry hairs. Front, back, top aslant, there is no angle that redeems swine. To God they're beautiful, I speculated, and screwed up my face, tried to imagine this God.

Amid muddy straw and squealing porkers, my mother stood in red pumps, lush crinolines radiating from her waist. Above the ruffles of her blouse she frowned at the nature of things: pigs were not to her liking. A spotted sow grunted, sniffing through the rails. Crudity for contrast, that must have been the reason, I decided. *This* God was more plausible, I could visualize him. He was educated, traveled, he loved beauty, and he had seen my mother. He had seen my mother bending to cultivate the base of lilies, walking down colonnades of wheat. *Too perfect*, he thought, it lacks complexity. Her alabaster countenance requires swine.

So he made pigs to set her off. I was happy with this explanation. She tugged at my sleeve, and we walked into starry dark, crossed to the produce building. Inside, I dawdled near Edith Bicrachek's embroidery. GOD BLESS THIS HOUSE. HE HELPS THOSE WHO HELP THEMSELVES. THE MEEK SHALL INHERIT THE EARTH. I leaned toward color, awed by fine

stitchery. But my mother read the words and became in-
censed. She squeezed my hand too tightly. My mother knew
which way the wind was blowing, and it was blowing out
from the plains toward both coasts, picking up houses,
factories, department stores, and drive-ins in its swirl and
depositing this architecture at the edge of both oceans. In
Seattle and Los Angeles men drove long silver cars; women
wore furs and danced to jazz. Clark Gable was somewhere in
one of those cities, and my father was even farther away. In
1947 the closest airport was in Chicago, nine hundred miles
away. She had seen film clips of U.S. Air Force planes
zooming for Tokyo, but she had never actually seen an
airplane. She was still stranded mid-continent, the biggest
news on the radio the market price of wheat.

Other mothers hoped to shield their daughters from
wickedness: mine would save me from perfect baking, the
bad influence of too much crochet. She whisked me past
Mason jars of Minnesota Wonders, hurried me out under the
expanse of stars. Her face was emblematic, a carved prow of
a Nordic ship stranded on land. She looked both ways, as
though expecting a stagecoach. She would invent some
fabulous vehicle for our escape.

"We'll ride the Ferris wheel," she announced. I could feel
her determination to rise above the toy shooting galleries, the
plain and flimsy people, this brief sprinkle of balloons. We
walked toward the revolving lights. My grandmother and
grandfather on the ground would dwindle, a little bride and
groom on a cake, and my mother and I would find the coast,
see Gable in the flesh, maybe even cross the ocean and find
my father. I would go with her up and out, step beside her onto
the radiant round. The pulsing hub would be our instrument.
My mother and I would make it in the sky.

But would we?
I kept up this fantasy as long as I could. Then, after a

while, I couldn't. Things were not so fine as they'd once been, and I had to acknowledge that this might be a message. Maybe progress was a pretense, maybe life was really a downward slipping.

But there ought to be one thing, I reasoned, just one thing each person could keep high up. In a motel in Nebraska I made my move. We were going to visit my cousins in Omaha, and Kovacs', for the moment, was behind us. It was late in the autumn, most of the leaves had fallen. I slept that night with her in the double bed, and when I woke in the morning and went to pee, I noticed the key in the bathroom door. It was a crude skeleton key, the lock the kind you can pick easily. I took the key back to the bed and examined it, turning it over and over, noticing its curious metallic smell, wondering if my mother would let me take it home. She lay in bed yawning and stretching while I tried the key in both sides of the bathroom door and in the front door keyhole. Then she sat up, went into the bathroom, turned on the shower.

I peeked through the keyhole. There she was, soaping herself under falling water, singing. Through the flimsy curtain I saw spray glancing off her back. She was still beautiful; it wasn't too late. There she was, slippery and precious to me, there was the key in my hand. It occurred to me that I could have what I wanted. I'd say, "Don't worry, I'll be right back." Then I'd take money from her purse, go out and buy mashed potatoes and gravy, sweet pickles, angel food cake. The thought of this food was exciting. Pickles! We'd laugh, and I would eat as many pickles as I wanted. I began to fiddle with the key, it turned easily. Then I tried the knob. The door was locked, I'd actually done it! I could keep her now as she should be kept, lovely and safe from work.

But as soon as I realized the bolt was really sunk, a terrible knowledge came to me: my mother would not be happy in this bathroom. She would not want to spend the rest of her life there, I was suddenly certain of this. Soon, very soon, she would want to come out and get dressed. I panicked, berating myself, fumbling to undo what I had done. The key turned easily, but now it would not turn back. I heard my mother turn off the shower, still singing. I sat down on the bed: at any moment she would try the door. The fact that my wish to keep her prisoner was ludicrous concerned me less at that moment than the fact that I could not perform the simple act of turning a key in a lock successfully. I sat, rigid, muscles constricting, shrinking with fear.

Still humming, she tried the door. "Honey?" she called.

"What," I said.

"Is the door locked?"

"Yes," I said. Both of us paused. Then my mother spoke.

"Well please unlock it, dear, I want to come out and get dressed."

I stood up, tried the key again. Again it would not turn. Though my fingers coaxed and twisted mightily, the key remained upright.

"I tried it before," I told her. "It won't."

"Well keep trying, honey," she said with elaborately casual patience. "You can do it." Her voice took on that quality of hoping to inspire the listener to confidence. This was a trick that had often worked with me before, but this time my mother's fear scared me. If she was afraid I couldn't do it, how could I possibly succeed?

I tried. Then I willed myself to simply disappear. Incapable of unlocking a door, incapable of magical disappearance. I was ruined, every way.

At some point my mother opened the window and began calling for help. I sat down on the bed again. What if help didn't come? What if it did? I longed for my shame to be over. But a flower picked could not be put back on its stem. What's done is done, my grandmother said as spilled milk spread across the tablecloth. I understood the finality of that statement.

9

The motel owner heard my mother's cries. When he knocked I let him in. He was a short man, and this increased my sense of my own ineptness. Even a short, not very spectacular man could perform the simple act of unlocking a door. For him the key turned easily. He tried the handle and the door swung open, revealing my mother wrapped in a white towel.

My mother looked at me. I was obliged to return her gaze. In a glance she assured me she believed this unfortunate incident was an accident. In a glance I assured her it would never happen again. She summoned her dignity and thanked the man. He assured her she had put him to no trouble, that in fact it had been his pleasure. He turned then and walked out, closing the door of our cabin behind him.

I have forgotten my cousins' faces, the feel of their beds, if it snowed. Back home my mother and I were different together. The snows were deep that year, and when I had to stay inside I tried to be careful. I did not march around bumping into things, leaving a trail of wreckage behind me. I tried to subdue my lust for pickles, and I certainly did not whine. I kept my voice mostly down, cultivating quiet. Quiet was my work now, like keeping my room neat before my grandmother told me to, or straightening the doilies on the backs of my grandmother's armchairs. I tried not to need much of anything beyond the bare necessities—food, clean clothes, a little conversation. I did not ask for ice cream or the privilege of staying up late. And I declined butcher paper, that extravagance I did not now deserve. I allowed myself only coloring books. And I stayed inside the lines.

One day when the snow had begun to melt and patches of brown grass were visible, my mother walked up to that table where I was coloring and put her hand on my shoulder. I was going methodically page by page through the book. Christmas was far in the past, but the picture before me was a poinsettia. It was that time between work and suppertime when there was still light but you knew that soon the light would go. "Have you noticed," she said, "that most of the snow is gone? Pretty soon those turtledoves will be looking for twigs, and the wasps will start building a nest." She walked to the kitchen and came back with a cylinder of butcher paper. Casually moving my coloring book aside, she unrolled it before me. "Let's color something big," she said.

I picked up a green crayon and made the ground. My mother began to draw a tree on her side, an elm leafing out, as the elms along the north side of our house would do, and I picked up purple and pink and orange and red and began to draw my mother. She was bigger than I'd ever drawn her, in a very full skirt and many crinolines, wonderfully fluffy hair and blue, blue eyes. I drew myself, too, smaller. Then I gave both of us high heels and put corsages on our shoulders. My mother was finishing a row of tulips. When she was done I put in the sun.

After that I began to pick up. I tried out my voice again, tinkered with the volume, tested the low and the high registers. My mother did not seem to mind. A little havoc seemed part of the natural order of things once again. More snow melted and the red tips of peony plants broke through the ground. Spring came on, and summer was coming. I began to allow my exuberance practically full play. I had my mother's good opinion, and I could not complain.

I had my mother's good opinion, but once in a while I felt the tug of sadness like the current of a slow but constant river. I had suffered my first great shame. After all, because of me she had had to stand naked, save for a narrow towel, before the eyes of a stranger.

Islands on the Moon

BARBARA KINGSOLVER

Annemarie's mother, Magda, is one of a kind. She wears sandals and one-hundred-percent-cotton dresses and walks like she's crossing plowed ground. She makes necklaces from the lacquered vertebrae of non-endangered species. Her hair is wavy and long and threaded with gray. She's forty-four.

Annemarie has always believed that if life had turned out better her mother would have been an artist. As it is, Magda just has to ooze out a little bit of art in everything she does, so that no part of her life is exactly normal. She paints landscapes on her tea kettles, for example, and dates younger men. Annemarie's theory is that everyone has some big thing, the rock in their road, that has kept them from greatness or so they would like to think. Magda had Annemarie when she was sixteen and has been standing on tiptoe ever since to see over or around her difficult daughter to whatever is on the other side. Annemarie just assumed that she was the rock in her mother's road. Until now. Now she has no idea.

On the morning Magda's big news arrived in the mail, Annemarie handed it over to her son Leon without even reading it, thinking it was just one of her standard cards. "Another magic message from Grandma Magda," she'd said, and Leon had rolled his eyes. He's nine years old, but that's only part of it. Annemarie influences him, telling my-most-embarrassing-moment stories about growing up with a mother like Magda, and Leon buys them wholesale, right along with nine-times-nine and the capital of Wyoming.

For example, Magda has always sent out winter solstice cards of her own design, printed on paper she makes by boiling down tree bark and weeds. The neighbors always smell it, and once, when Annemarie was a teenager, they reported Magda as a nuisance.

But it's April now so this isn't a solstice card. It's not homemade, either. It came from one of those stores where you can buy a personalized astrology chart for a baby gift. The paper is yellowed and smells of incense. Leon holds it to his nose, then turns it in his hands, not trying to decipher Magda's slanty handwriting but studying the ink drawing that runs around the border. Leon has curly black hair, like Magda's — and like Annemarie's would be, if she didn't continually crop it and bleach it and wax it into spikes. But Leon doesn't care who he looks like. He's entirely unconscious of himself as he sits there, ears sticking out, heels banging the stool at the kitchen counter. One of Annemarie's cats rubs the length of its spine along his green hightop sneaker.

"It looks like those paper dolls that come out all together, holding hands," he says. "Only they're fattish, like old ladies. Dancing."

"That's about what I'd decided," says Annemarie.

Leon hands the card back and heads for fresh air. The bang of the screen door is the closest she gets these days to a goodbye kiss.

Where, in a world where kids play with Masters of the Universe, has Leon encountered holding-hands paper dolls? This is what disturbs Annemarie. Her son is normal in every obvious way but has a freakish awareness of old-fashioned things. He collects things: old Coke bottles, license-plate slogans, anything. They'll be driving down Broadway and he'll call out "Illinois Land of Lincoln!" And he saves string. Annemarie found it in a ball, rolled into a sweatsock. It's as if some whole piece of Magda has come through to Leon without even touching her.

She reads the card and stares at the design, numb, trying to see what these little fat dancing women have to be happy about. She and her mother haven't spoken for months, although either one can see the other's mobile home when she steps out on the porch to shake the dust mop. Magda says she's willing to wait until Annemarie stops emitting negative energy toward her. In the meantime she sends cards.

Annemarie is suddenly stricken, as she often is, with the feeling she's about to be abandoned. Leon will take Magda's side. He'll think this new project of hers is great, and mine's awful. Magda always wins without looking like she was trying.

Annemarie stands at the kitchen sink staring out the window at her neighbor's porch, which is twined with queen's wreath and dusty honeysuckle, a stalwart oasis in the desert of the trailer court. A plaster Virgin Mary, painted in blue and rose and the type of cheap, shiny gold that chips easily, presides over the barbecue pit, and three lawn chairs with faded webbing are drawn up close around it as if for some secret family ceremony. A wooden sign hanging from the porch awning proclaims that they are "Navarrete's" over there. Their grandson, who lives with them, made the sign in Boy Scouts. Ten years Annemarie has been trying to get out of this trailer court, and the people next door are so content with themselves they hang out a shingle.

Before she knows it she's crying, wiping her face with the backs of her dishpan hands. This is completely normal. All morning she sat by herself watching nothing in particular on TV, and cried when Luis and Maria got married on *Sesame Street*. It's the hormones. She hasn't told him yet, but she's going to have another child besides Leon. The big news in Magda's card is that she is going to have another child too, besides Annemarie.

When she tries to be reasonable — and she is trying at the moment, sitting in a Denny's with her best friend Kay Kay — Annemarie knows that mid-forties isn't too old to have boyfriends. But Magda doesn't seem mid-forties, she seems like Grandma Moses in moonstone earrings. She's the type who's proud about not having to go to the store for some little thing because she can rummage around in the kitchen drawers until she finds some other thing that will serve just as well. For her fifth birthday Annemarie screamed for a Bubble-Hairdo Barbie just because she knew there wouldn't be one in the kitchen drawer.

Annemarie's side of the story is that she had to fight her way out of a family that smelled like an old folks' home. Her father was devoted and funny, chasing her around the house after dinner in white paper-napkin masks with eye-holes, and he could fix anything on wheels, and then without warning he turned into a wheezing old man with taut-skinned hands rattling a bottle of pills. Then he was dead, leaving behind a medicinal pall that hung over Annemarie and followed her to school. They'd saved up just enough to move to Tucson, for his lungs, and the injustice of it stung her. He'd breathed the scorched desert air for a single autumn, and Annemarie had to go on breathing it one summer after another. In New Hampshire she'd had friends, as many as the trees had leaves, but they couldn't get back there now. Magda was vague and useless, no protection from poverty. Only fathers, it seemed,

15

offered that particular safety. Magda reminded her that the Little Women were poor too, and for all practical purposes fatherless, but Annemarie didn't care. The March girls didn't have to live in a trailer court.

Eventually Magda went on dates. By that time Annemarie was sneaking Marlboros and fixing her hair and hanging around by the phone, and would have given her eyeteeth for as many offers — but Magda threw them away. Even back then, she didn't get attached to men. She devoted herself instead to saving every rubber band and piece of string that entered their door. Magda does the things people used to do in other centuries, before it occurred to them to pay someone else to do them. Annemarie's friends think this is wonderful. Magda is so old-fashioned she's come back into style. And she's committed. She intends to leave her life savings, if any, to Save the Planet, and tells Annemarie she should be more concerned about the stewardship of the earth. Kay Kay thinks she ought to be the president. "You want to trade?" she routinely asks. "You want my mother?"

"What's wrong with your mother?" Annemarie wants to know.

"What's wrong with my mother," Kay Kay answers, shaking her head. Everybody thinks they've got a corner on the market, thinks Annemarie.

Kay Kay is five feet two and has green eyes and drives a locomotive for Southern Pacific. She's had the same lover, a rock 'n' roll singer named Connie Skylab, for as long as Annemarie has known her. Kay Kay and Connie take vacations that just amaze Annemarie: they'll go skiing, or hang-gliding, or wind-surfing down in Puerto Peñasco. Annemarie often wishes she could do just one brave thing in her lifetime. Like hang-gliding.

"Okay, here you go," says Kay Kay. "For my birthday my mother sent me one of those fold-up things you carry in your purse for covering up the toilet seat. 'Honey, you're on the go so much,' she says to me. 'And besides there's AIDS to think about now.' The guys at work think I ought to have it bronzed."

"At least she didn't try to *knit* you a toilet-seat cover, like Magda would," says Annemarie. "She bought it at a store, right?"

"Number one," Kay Kay says, "I don't carry a purse when I'm driving a train. And number two, I don't know how to tell Ma this, but the bathrooms in those engines don't even *have* a seat."

Annemarie and Kay Kay are having lunch. Kay Kay spends her whole life in restaurants when she isn't driving a train. She says if you're going to pull down thirty-eight thousand a year, why cook?

"At least you had a normal childhood," Annemarie says, taking a mirror-compact out of her purse, confirming that she looks awful, and snapping it shut. "I was the only teenager in America that couldn't use hairspray because it's death to the ozone layer."

"I just don't see what's so terrible about Magda caring what happens to the world," Kay Kay says.

"It's morbid. All those war marches she goes on. How can you think all the time about nuclear winter wiping out life as we know it, and still go on making your car payments?"

Kay Kay smiles.

"She mainly just does it to remind me what a slug I am. I didn't turn out all gung-ho like she wanted me to."

"That's not true," Kay Kay says. "You're very responsible, in your way. I think Magda just wants a safe world for you and Leon. My mother couldn't care less if the world went to hell in a handbasket, as long as her nail color was coordinated with her lipstick."

Annemarie can never make people see. She cradles her chin mournfully in her palms. Annemarie has surprisingly fair skin for a black-haired person, which she is in principle.

That particular complexion, from Magda's side of the family, has dropped unaltered through the generations like a rock. They are fine-boned, too, with graceful necks and fingers that curve outward slightly at the tips. Annemarie had wished for awful things in her lifetime, even stubby fingers, something to set her apart.

"I got my first period," she tells Kay Kay, unable to drop the subject, "at this *die-in* she organized against the Vietnam War. I had horrible cramps and nobody paid any attention; they all thought I was just dying-in."

"And you're never going to forgive her," Kay Kay says. "You ought to have a T-shirt made up: 'I hate my mother because I got my first period at a die-in.'"

Annemarie attends to her salad, which she has no intention of eating. Two tables away, a woman in a western shirt and heavy turquoise jewelry is watching Annemarie in a maternal way over her husband's shoulder. "She just has to one-up me," says Annemarie. "Her due date is a month before mine."

"I can see where you'd be upset," Kay Kay says, "but she didn't know. You didn't even tell me till a month ago. It's not like she grabbed some guy off the street and said, 'Quick, knock me up so I can steal my daughter's thunder.'"

Annemarie doesn't like to think about Magda having sex with some guy off the street. "She should have an abortion," she says. "Childbirth is unsafe at her age."

"Your mother can't part with the rubber band off the Sunday paper."

This is true. Annemarie picks off the alfalfa sprouts, which she didn't ask for in the first place. Magda used to make her wheat-germ sandwiches, knowing full well she despised sprouts and anything else that was recently a seed. Annemarie is crying now and there's no disguising it. She was still a kid when she had Leon, but this baby she'd intended to do on her own. With a man maybe, but not with her mother prancing around on center stage.

"Lots of women have babies in their forties," Kay Kay says. "Look at Goldie Hawn."

"Goldie Hawn isn't my mother. *And* she's married."

"Is the father that guy I met? Bartholomew?"

"The father is not in the picture. That's a quote. You know Magda and men; she's not going to let the grass grow under *her* bed."

Kay Kay is looking down at her plate, using her knife and fork in a serious way that shows all the tendons in her hands. Kay Kay generally argues with Annemarie only if she's putting herself down. When she starts in on Magda, Kay Kay mostly just listens.

"Ever since Daddy died she's never looked back," Annemarie says, blinking. Her contact lenses are foundering, like skaters on a flooded rink.

"And you think she ought to look back?"

"I don't know. Yeah." She dabs at her eyes, trying not to look at the woman with the turquoise bracelets. "It bothers me. Bartholomew's in love with her. Another guy wants to marry her. All these guys are telling her how beautiful she is. And look at me, it seems like every year I'm crying over another boyfriend gone west, not even counting Leon's dad." She takes a bite of lettuce and chews on empty calories. "I'm still driving the Pontiac I bought ten years ago, but I've gone through six boyfriends and a husband. Twice. I was married to Buddy twice."

"Well, look at it this way, at least you've got a good car," says Kay Kay.

"Now that this kid's on the way he's talking about going for marriage number three. Him and Leon are in cahoots, I think."

"You and Buddy again?"

"Buddy's settled down a lot," Annemarie insists. "I think I could get him to stay home more this time." Buddy wears braids like his idol, Willie Nelson, and drives a car with flames painted on the hood. When Annemarie says he has settled down, she means that whereas he used to try to avoid work in his father's lawnmower repair shop, now he owns it.

"Maybe it would be good for Leon. A boy needs his dad."

"Oh, Leon's a rock, like me," says Annemarie. "It comes from growing up alone. When I try to do any little thing for Leon he acts like I'm the creature from the swamp. I know he'd rather live with Buddy. He'll be out the door for good one of these days."

"Well, you never know, it might work out with you and Buddy," Kay Kay says brightly. "Maybe third time's a charm."

"Oh, sure. Seems like guys want to roll through my life like the drive-in window. Probably me and Buddy'll end up going for divorce number three." She pulls a paper napkin out of the holder and openly blows her nose.

"Why don't you take the afternoon off?" Kay Kay suggests. "Go home and take a nap. I'll call your boss for you, and tell him you've got afternoon sickness or something."

Annemarie visibly shrugs off Kay Kay's concern. "Oh, I couldn't, he'd kill me. I'd better get back." Annemarie is assistant manager of a discount delivery service called "Yesterday!" and really holds the place together, though she denies it.

"Well, don't get down in the dumps," says Kay Kay gently. "You've just got the baby blues."

"If it's not one kind of blues it's another. I can't help it. Just the sound of the word 'divorced' makes me feel like I'm dragging around a suitcase of dirty handkerchiefs."

Kay Kay nods.

"The thing that gets me about Magda is, man or no man, it's all the same to her," Annemarie explains, feeling the bitterness of this truth between her teeth like a sour apple. "When it comes to men, she doesn't even carry any luggage."

The woman in the turquoise bracelets stops watching Annemarie and gets up to go to the restroom. The husband, whose back is turned, waits for the bill.

The telephone wakes Annemarie. It's not late, only a little past seven, the sun is still up, and she's confused. She must have fallen asleep without meaning to. She is cut through with terror while she struggles to place where Leon is and remember whether he's been fed. Since his birth, falling asleep in the daytime has served up to Annemarie this momentary shock of guilt.

When she hears the voice on the phone and understands who it is, she stares at the receiver, thinking somehow that it's not her phone. She hasn't heard her mother's voice for such a long time.

"All I'm asking is for you to go with me to the clinic," Magda is saying. "You don't have to look at the needle. You don't even have to hold my hand." She waits, but Annemarie is speechless. "You don't even have to talk to me. Just peck on the receiver: once if you'll go, twice if you won't." Magda is trying to sound light-hearted, but Annemarie realizes with a strange satisfaction that she must be very afraid. She's going to have amniocentesis.

"Are you all right?" Magda asks. "You sound woozy."

"Why wouldn't I be all right," Annemarie snaps. She runs a hand through her hair, which is spiked with perspiration, and regains herself. "Why on earth are you even having it done, the amniowhatsis, if you think it's going to be so awful?"

"My doctor won't be my doctor anymore unless I have it. It's kind of a requirement for women my age."

A yellow tabby cat walks over Annemarie's leg and jumps off the bed. Annemarie is constantly taking in strays, joking to Kay Kay that if Leon leaves her at least she won't be alone, she'll have the cats. She has eleven or twelve at the moment.

"Well, it's probably for the best," Annemarie tells Magda, in the brisk voice she uses to let Magda know she is a citizen of the world, unlike some people. "It will ease your mind, anyway, to know the baby's okay."

"Oh, I'm not going to look at the results," Magda explains. "I told Dr. Lavinna I'd have it, and have the results sent over to his office, but I don't want to know. That was our compromise."

"Why don't you want to know the results?" asks Annemarie. "You could even know if it was a boy or a girl. You could pick out a name."

"As if it's such hard work to pick out an extra name," says Magda, "that I should go have needles poked into me to save myself the trouble?"

"I just don't see why you wouldn't want to know."

"People spend their whole lives with labels stuck on them, Annemarie. I just think it would be nice for this one to have nine months of being a plain human being."

"Mother knows best," sighs Annemarie, and she has the feeling she's always had, that she's sinking in a bog of mud. "You two should just talk," Kay Kay sometimes insists, and Annemarie can't get across that it's like quicksand. It's like reasoning with the sand trap at a golf course. There is no beginning and no end to the conversation she needs to have with Magda, and she'd rather just steer clear.

The following day, after work, Kay Kay comes over to help Annemarie get her evaporative cooler going for the summer. It's up on the roof of her mobile home. They have to climb up there with the vacuum cleaner and a long extension cord and clean out a winter's worth of dust and twigs and wayward insect parts. Then they will paint the bottom of the tank with tar, and install new pads, and check the water lines. Afterward, Kay Kay has promised she'll take

Annemarie to the Dairy Queen for a milkshake. Kay Kay is looking after her friend in a carefully offhand way that Annemarie hasn't quite noticed.

It actually hasn't dawned on Annemarie that she's halfway through a pregnancy. She just doesn't think about what's going on in there, other than having some vague awareness that someone has moved in and is rearranging the furniture of her body. She's been thinking mostly about what pants she can still fit into. It was this way the first time, too. At six months she marched with Buddy down the aisle in an empire gown and seed-pearl tiara and no one suspected a thing, including, in her heart-of-hearts, Annemarie. Seven weeks later Leon sprang out of her body with his mouth open, already yelling, and neither one of them has ever quite gotten over the shock.

It's not that she doesn't want this baby, she tells Kay Kay; she didn't at first, but now she's decided. Leon has reached the age where he dodges her kisses like wild pitches over home plate, and she could use someone around to cuddle. "But there are so many things I have to get done, before I can have it," she says.

"Like what kind of things?" Kay Kay has a bandanna tied around her head and is slapping the tar around energetically. She's used to dirty work. She says after you've driven a few hundred miles with your head out the window of a locomotive, you don't just take a washcloth to your face, you have to wash your *teeth*.

"Oh, I don't know." Annemarie sits back on her heels. The metal roof is too hot to touch, but the view from up there is interesting, almost like it's not where she lives. The mobile homes are arranged like shoeboxes along the main drive, with cars and motorbikes parked beside them, just so many toys in a sandbox. The shadows of things trail away everywhere in the same direction like long oil leaks across the gravel. The trailer court is called "Island Breezes," and like the names of most trailer courts, it's a joke. No swaying palm trees. In fact, there's no official vegetation at all except for cactus plants in straight, symmetrical rows along the drive, like some bizarre desert organized by a child.

"Well, deciding what to do about Buddy, for instance," Annemarie says at last, after Kay Kay has clearly forgotten the question. "I need to figure that out first. And also what I'd do with a baby while I'm at work. I couldn't leave it with Magda, they'd all be down at the Air Force Base getting arrested to stop the cruise missiles."

Kay Kay doesn't say anything. She wraps the tarred, spiky paintbrush in a plastic bag and begins to pry last year's cooler pads out of the frames. Annemarie is being an absent-minded helper, staring into space, sometimes handing Kay Kay a screwdriver when she's asked for the pliers.

With a horrible screeching of claws on metal, one of Annemarie's cats, Lone Ranger, has managed to get himself up to the roof in pursuit of a lizard. He's surprised to see the women up there; he freezes and then slinks away along the gutter. Lone Ranger is a problem cat. Annemarie buys him special food, anything to entice him, but he won't come inside and be pampered. He cowers and shrinks from love like a blast from the hose.

"How long you think you'll take off work?" Kay Kay asks.

"Take off?"

"When the baby comes."

"Oh, I don't know," Annemarie says, uneasily. She could endanger her job there if she doesn't give them some kind of advance notice. She's well aware, even when Kay Kay refrains from pointing it out, that she's responsible in a hit-or-miss way. Once, toward the end of their first marriage, Buddy totaled his car and she paid to have it repaired so he wouldn't leave her. The next weekend he drove to Reno with a woman who sold newspapers from a traffic island.

Annemarie begins to unwrap the new cooler pads, which look like huge, flat sponges and smell like fresh sawdust. According to the label they're made of aspen, which Annemarie thought was a place you go skiing and try to get a glimpse of Jack Nicholson. "You'd think they could make these things out of plastic," she says. "They'd last longer, and it wouldn't smell like a damn camping trip every time you turn on your cooler."

"They have to absorb water, though," explains Kay Kay. "That's the whole point. When the fan blows through the wet pads it cools down the air."

Annemarie is in the mood where she can't get particularly interested in the way things work. She holds two of the pads against herself like a hula skirt. "I could see these as a costume, couldn't you? For Connie?"

"That's an idea," Kay Kay says, examining them thoughtfully. "Connie's allergic to grasses, but not wood fibers."

Annemarie's bones ache to be known and loved this well. What she wouldn't give for someone to stand on a roof, halfway across the city, and say to some other person, "Annemarie's allergic to grasses, but not wood fibers."

"I'll mention it," Kay Kay says. "The band might go for it." Connie Skylab and the Falling Debris are into outlandish looks. Connie performs one number, "My Mother's Teeth," dressed in a black plastic garbage bag and a necklace of sheep's molars. A line Annemarie remembers is: "My mother's teeth grow in my head, I'll eat my children's dreams when she is dead."

Connie's mother is, in actual fact, dead. But neither she nor Kay Kay plans to produce any children. Annemarie thinks maybe that's how they can be so happy and bold. Their relationship is a sleek little boat of their own construction, untethered in either direction by the knotted ropes of motherhood, free to sail the open seas. Some people can manage it. Annemarie once met a happily married couple who made jewelry and traveled the nation in a dented microbus, selling their wares on street corners. They had no permanent address whatsoever, no traditions, no family. They told Annemarie they never celebrated holidays.

And then on the other hand there are the Navarretes next door with their little nest of lawn chairs. They're happy too. Annemarie feels permanently disqualified from either camp, the old-fashioned family or the new. It's as if she somehow got left behind, missed every boat across the river, and now must watch happiness being acted out on the beach of a distant shore.

Two days later, on Saturday, Annemarie pulls on sweat pants and a T-shirt, starts up her Pontiac — scattering cats in every direction — and drives a hundred feet to pick up Magda and take her to the clinic. There just wasn't any reasonable way out.

The sun is reflected so brightly off the road it's like driving on a mirage. The ground is as barren as some planet where it rains once per century. It has been an unusually dry spring, though it doesn't much matter here in Island Breezes, where the lawns are made of gravel. Some people, deeply missing the Midwest, have spray-painted their gravel green.

Magda's yard is naturally the exception. It's planted with many things, including clumps of aloevera, which she claims heals burns, and most recently, a little hand-painted sign with a blue dove that explains to all and sundry passers-by that you can't hug your kids with nuclear arms. When Annemarie drives up, Magda's standing out on the wooden steps in one of her loose India-print cotton dresses, and looks cool. Annemarie is envious. Magda's ordinary wardrobe will carry her right through the ninth month.

Magda's hair brushes her shoulders like a lace curtain as she gets into the car, and she seems flushed and excited, though perhaps it's nerves. She fishes around in her enormous woven bag and pulls out a bottle of green shampoo. "I thought you might like to try this. It has an extract of nettles. I know to you that probably sounds awful, but it's really good; it can repair damaged hair shafts."

Annemarie beeps impatiently at some kids playing kickball in the drive near the front entrance. "Magda, can we please not start right in *immediately* on my hair? Can we at least say, 'How do you do' and 'Fine thank you' before we start in on my hair?"

"Sorry."

"Believe it or not, I actually *want* my hair to look like something dead beside the road. It's the style now."

Magda looks around behind the seat for the seat belt and buckles it up. She refrains from saying anything about Annemarie's seat belt. They literally don't speak again until they get where they're going.

At the clinic they find themselves listening to a lecture on AIDS prevention. Apparently it's a mandatory part of the services here. Before Magda's amniocentesis they need to sit with the other patients and learn about nonoxynol-number-9 spermicide and the proper application of a condom.

"You want to leave a little room at the end, like this," says the nurse, who's wearing jeans and red sneakers. She rolls the condom carefully onto a plastic banana. All the other people in the room look fourteen, and there are some giggles. Their mothers probably go around saying that they and their daughters are "close," and have no idea they're here today getting birth control and what not.

Finally Magda gets to see the doctor, but it's a more complicated procedure than Annemarie expected: first they have to take a sonogram, to make sure that when they stick in the needle they won't poke the baby.

"Even if that did happen," the doctor explains, "the fetus will usually just move out of the way." Annemarie is floored

27

to imagine a five-month-old fetus fending for itself. She tries to think of what's inside her as being an actual baby, or a baby-to-be, but can't. She hasn't even felt it move yet.

The doctor rubs Magda's belly with Vaseline and then places against it something that looks like a Ping-Pong paddle wired for sound. She frowns at the TV screen, concentrating, and then points. "Look, there, you can see the head."

Magda and Annemarie watch a black-and-white screen where meaningless shadows move around each other like iridescent ink blots. Suddenly they can make out one main shadow, fish-shaped with a big head, like Casper the Friendly Ghost.

"The bladder's full," the doctor says. "See that little clear spot? That's a good sign, it means the kidneys are working. Oops, there it went."

"There what went?" asks Magda.

"The bladder. It voided." She looks closely at the screen, smiling. "You know, I can't promise you but I think what you've got here . . ."

"Don't tell me," Magda says. "If you're going to tell me if it's a boy or a girl, I don't want to know."

"I do," says Annemarie. "Tell me."

"Is that okay with you?" the doctor asks Magda, and Magda shrugs. "Close your eyes, then," she tells Magda. She holds up two glass tubes with rubber stoppers, one pink and the other blue-green. She nods at the pink one.

Annemarie smiles. "Okay, all clear," she tells Magda. "My lips are sealed."

"That's the face, right there," the doctor says, pointing out the eyes. "It has one fist in its mouth; that's very common at this stage. Can you see it?"

They can see it. The other fist, the left one, is raised up alongside its huge head like the Black Panther salute. Magda is transfixed. Annemarie can see the flickering light of the screen reflected in her eyes, and she understands for the first time that what they are looking at here is not a plan or a plot, it has nothing to do with herself. It's Magda's future.

Afterward they have to go straight to the park to pick up Leon from softball practice. It's hot, and Annemarie drives distractedly, worrying about Leon because they're late. She talked him into joining the league in the first place; he'd just as soon stay home and collect baseball cards. But now she worries that he'll get hit with a ball, or kidnapped by some pervert that hangs around in the park waiting for the one little boy whose mother's late. She hits the brakes at a crosswalk to let three women pass safely through the traffic, walking with their thin brown arms so close together they could be holding hands. They're apparently three generations of a family: the grandmother is draped elaborately in a sari, the mother is in pink slacks, and the daughter wears a bleached denim miniskirt. But from the back they could be triplets. Three long braids, woven as thin and tight as ropes, bounce placidly against their backs as they walk away from the stopped cars.

"Was it as bad as you thought it would be?" Annemarie asks Magda. It's awkward to be speaking after all this time, so suddenly, and really for no good reason.

"It was worse."

"I liked the sonogram," Annemarie says. "I liked seeing it, didn't you?"

"Yes, but not that other part. I hate doctors and needles and that whole thing. Doctors treat women like a disease in progress."

That's Magda, Annemarie thinks. You never know what's going to come out of her mouth next. Annemarie thinks the doctor was just about as nice as possible. But in fairness to Magda, the needle was unbelievably long. It made her skin draw up into goose pimples just to watch. Magda seems worn out from the experience.

Annemarie rolls down the window to signal a left turn at the intersection. Her blinkers don't work, but at least the air conditioning still does. In the summer when her mobile home heats up like a toaster oven, the car is Annemarie's refuge. Sometimes she'll drive across town on invented, insignificant errands, singing along with Annie Lennox on the radio and living for the moment in a small, safe, perfectly cool place.

"I'd have this baby at home if I could," says Magda.

"Why can't you?"

"Too old," she says, complacently. "I talked to the midwife program but they risked me out."

The sun seems horribly bright. Annemarie thinks she's read something about pregnancy making your eyes sensitive to light. "Was it an awful shock, when they found out?" she asks Magda.

"About the midwives?"

"No. About the pregnancy."

Magda looks at her as if she's dropped from another planet.

"What's the matter?" asks Annemarie.

"I've been trying my whole life to have more babies. You knew that, that I'd been trying."

"No, I didn't. Just lately?"

"No, Annemarie, not just lately, forever. The whole time with your father we kept trying, but the drugs he took for the cancer knocked out his sperms. The doctor told us they were still alive, but were too confused to make a baby."

Annemarie tries not to smile. "Too confused?"

"That's what he said."

"And you've kept on ever since then?" she asks.

"I kept hoping, but I'd about given up. I feel like this baby is a gift."

Annemarie thinks of one of the customers at Yesterday!

who sent relatives a Christmas fruitcake that somehow got lost; it arrived two and a half years later on the twelfth of July. Magda's baby is like the fruitcake, she thinks, and she shakes her head and laughs.

"What's so funny?"

"Nothing. I just can't believe you wanted a bunch of kids. You never said so. I thought even having just me got in your way."

"Got in my way?"

"Well, yeah. Because you were so young. I thought that's why you weren't mad when Buddy and I had to get married, because you'd done the same thing. I always figured my middle name ought to have been Whoops."

Magda looks strangely at Annemarie again. "I had to douche with vinegar to get pregnant with you," she says.

They've reached the park, and Leon is waiting with his bat slung over his shoulder like a dangerous character. "The other kids' moms already came ten hours ago," he says when he gets into the car. He doesn't seem at all surprised to see Magda and Annemarie in the same vehicle.

"We got held up," Annemarie says. "Sorry, Leon."

Leon stares out the window for a good while. "Leon's a stupid name," he says, eventually. This is a complaint of his these days.

"There have been a lot of important Leons in history," Annemarie says.

"Like who?"

She considers this. "Leon Russell," she says. "He's a rock and roll singer."

"Leon Trotsky," says Magda.

Annemarie has heard all about Leon Trotsky in her time, and Rosa Luxemburg, and Mother Jones.

"Trotsky was an important socialist who disagreed with Stalin's methodology," Magda explains. "Stalin was the kingpin at the time, so Trotsky had to run for his life to

Mexico."

"This all happened decades ago, I might add," Annemarie says, glancing at Leon in the rear-view mirror.

"He was killed by his trusted secretary," Magda continues. "With an axe in the head."

"Magda, please. You think he'll like his name better if he knows many famous Leons have been axed?"

"I'm telling him my girlhood memories. I'm trying to be a good grandmother."

"Your girlhood memories? What, were you there?"

"Of course not, it happened in Mexico, before I was born. But it affected me. I read about it when I was a teenager, and I cried. My father said, 'Oh, I remember seeing that headline in the paper and thinking, What, Trotsky's dead? *Hal* Trotsky, first baseman for the Cleveland Indians?'"

"Live Free or Die, New Hampshire!" shouts Leon at an approaching car.

Magda says, "Annemarie's father came from New Hampshire."

Annemarie runs a stop sign.

It isn't clear to her what's happened. There is a crunch of metal and glass, and some white thing plowing like a torpedo into the left side of the Pontiac, and they spin around, seeing the same view pass by again and again. Then Annemarie is lying across Magda with her mouth open and her head out the window on the passenger's side. Magda's arms are tight around her chest. The window has vanished, and there is a feeling like sand trickling through Annemarie's hair. After a minute she realizes that a sound is coming out of her mouth. It's a scream. She closes her mouth and it stops.

With some effort she unbuckles Magda's seat belt and pulls the door handle and they more or less tumble out together onto the ground. It strikes Annemarie, for no good reason, that Magda isn't a very big person. She's Annemarie's own size, if not smaller. The sun is unbelievably bright.

There's no other traffic. A woman gets out of the white car with the New Hampshire plates, brushing her beige skirt in a businesslike way and straightening her hair. Oddly, she has on stockings but no shoes. She looks at the front end of her car, which resembles a metal cauliflower, and then at the two women hugging each other on the ground.

"There was a stop sign," she says. Her voice is clear as a song in the strange silence. A series of rapid clicks emanates from the underside of one of the cars, then stops.

"I guess I missed it," Annemarie says.

"Are you okay?" the woman asks. She looks hard at Annemarie's face. Annemarie puts her hand on her head, and it feels wet.

"I'm fine," she and Magda say at the same time.

"You're bleeding," the woman says to Annemarie. She looks down at herself, and then carefully unbuttons her white blouse and holds it out to Annemarie. "You'd better let me tie this around your head," she says. "Then I'll go call the police."

"All right," says Annemarie. She pries apart Magda's fingers, which seem to be stuck, and they pull each other up. The woman pulls the blouse across Annemarie's bleeding forehead and knots the silk sleeves tightly at the nape of her neck. She does this while standing behind Annemarie in her stocking feet and brassiere, with Magda looking on, and somehow it has the feeling of some ordinary female ritual.

"Oh, God," says Annemarie. She looks at the Pontiac and sits back down on the ground. The back doors of the car are standing wide open, and Leon is gone. "My son," she says. The child inside her flips and arches its spine in a graceful, hungry movement, like a dolphin leaping for a fish held out by its tail.

"Is that him?" the woman asks, pointing to the far side of the intersection. Leon is there, sitting cross-legged on a mound of dirt. On one side of him there is a jagged pile of broken cement. On the other side is a stack of concrete pipes. Leon looks at his mother and grandmother, and laughs.

Annemarie can't stop sobbing in the back of the ambulance. She knows that what she's feeling would sound foolish put into words: that there's no point in living once you understand that at any moment you could die.

She and Magda are strapped elaborately onto boards, so they can't turn their heads even to look at each other. Magda says over and over again, "Leon's okay. You're okay. We're all okay." Out the window Annemarie can only see things that are high up: telephone wires, clouds, an airplane full of people who have no idea how near they could be to death. Daily there are reports of mid-air collisions barely averted. When the ambulance turns a corner she can see the permanent landmark of the Catalina Mountains standing over the city. In a saddle between two dark peaks a storm cloud spreads out like a fan, and Annemarie sees how easily it could grow into something else, tragically roiling up into itself, veined with blinding light: a mushroom cloud.

"Magda," she says, "me too. I'm having a baby too."

At the hospital Magda repeats to everyone, like a broken record, that she and her daughter are both pregnant. She's terrified they'll be given some tranquilizer that will mutate the fetuses. Whenever the nurses approach, she confuses them by talking about Thalidomide babies. "Annemarie is allergic to penicillin," she warns the doctor when they're separated. It's true, Annemarie is, and she always forgets to mark it on her forms.

It turns out that she needs no penicillin, just stitches in her scalp. Magda has cuts and serious contusions from where her knees hit the dash. Leon has nothing. Not a bruise.

During the lecture the doctor gives them about seat belts, which Annemarie will remember for the rest of her life, he explains that in an average accident the human body becomes as heavy as a piano dropping from a ten-story building. She has bruises on her rib cage from where Magda held on to her, and the doctor can't understand how she kept Annemarie from going out the window. He looks at the two of them, pregnant and dazed, and tells them many times over that they are two very lucky ladies. "Sometimes the strength of motherhood is greater than natural laws," he declares.

The only telephone number Annemarie can think to give them is the crew dispatcher for Southern Pacific, which is basically Kay Kay's home number. Luckily she's just brought in the Amtrak and is next door to the depot, at Wendy's, when the call comes. She gets there in minutes, still dressed in her work boots and blackened jeans, with a green bandanna around her neck.

"They didn't want me to come in here," Kay Kay tells Annemarie in the recovery room. "They said I was too dirty. Can you imagine?"

Annemarie tries to laugh, but tears run from her eyes instead, and she squeezes Kay Kay's hand. She still can't think of anything that seems important enough to say. She feels as if life has just been handed to her in a heavy and formal way, like a microphone on a stage, and the audience is waiting to see what great thing she intends to do with it.

But Kay Kay is her everyday self. "Don't worry about Leon, he's got it all worked out, he's staying with me," she tells Annemarie, not looking at her stitches. "He's going to teach me how to hit a softball."

"He doesn't want to go to Buddy's?" Annemarie asks.

"He didn't say he did."

"Isn't he scared to death?" Annemarie feels so weak and confused she doesn't believe she'll ever stand up again.

Kay Kay smiles. "Leon's a rock," she says, and Annemarie thinks of the pile of dirt he landed on. She believes now that she can remember the sound of him hitting it.

Annemarie and Magda have to stay overnight for observation. They end up in maternity, with their beds pushed close together so they won't disturb the other woman in the room. She's just given birth to twins and is watching *Falcon Crest*.

"I just keep seeing him there on that pile of dirt," whispers Annemarie. "And I think, he could have been dead. There was just that one little safe place for him to land. Why did he land there? And then I think, *we* could have been dead, and he'd be alone. He'd be an orphan. Like that poor little girl that survived that plane wreck."

"That poor kid," Magda agrees. "People are just burying her with teddy bears. How could you live with a thing like that?" Magda seems a little dazed too. They each accepted a pill to calm them down, once the doctor came and personally guaranteed Magda it wouldn't cause fetal deformity.

"I think that woman's blouse was silk. Can you believe it?" Annemarie asks.

"She was kind," says Magda.

"I wonder what became of it? I suppose it's ruined."

"Probably," Magda says. She keeps looking over at Annemarie and smiling. "When are you due?" she asks.

"October twelfth," says Annemarie. "After you."

"Leon came early, remember. And I went way late with you, three weeks I think. Yours could come first."

"Did you know Buddy wants us to get married again?" Annemarie asks after a while. "Leon thinks it's a great idea."

"What do you think? That's the question."

"That's the question," Annemarie agrees.

A nurse comes to take their blood pressure. "How are the mamas tonight?" she asks. Annemarie thinks about how nurses wear that same calm face stewardesses have, never letting on like you're sitting on thirty thousand feet of thin air. Her head has begun to ache in no uncertain terms, and she thinks of poor old Leon Trotsky, axed in the head.

"I dread to think of what my hair's going to look like when

these bandages come off. Did they have to shave a lot?"

"Not too much," the nurse says, concentrating on the blood-pressure dial.

"Well, it's just as well my hair was a wreck to begin with."

The nurse smiles and rips off the Velcro cuff, and then turns her back on Annemarie, attending to Magda. Another nurse rolls in their dinners and sets up their tray tables. Magda props herself up halfway, grimacing a little, and the nurse helps settle her with pillows under her back. She pokes a straw into a carton of milk, but Annemarie doesn't even take the plastic wrap off her tray.

"Ugh," she complains, once the nurses have padded away on their white soles. "This reminds me of the stuff you used to bring me when I was sick."

"Milk toast," says Magda.

"That's right. Toast soaked in milk. Who could dream up such a disgusting thing?"

"I like it," says Magda. "When I'm sick, it's the only thing I can stand. Seems like it always goes down nice."

"It went down nice with Blackie," Annemarie says. "Did you know he's the one that always ate it? I told you a million times I hated milk toast."

"I never knew what you expected from me, Annemarie. I never could be the mother you wanted."

Annemarie turns up one corner of the cellophane and pleats it with her fingers. "I guess I didn't expect anything, and you kept giving it to me anyway. When I was a teenager you were always making me drink barley fiber so I wouldn't have colon cancer when I was fifty. All I wanted was Cokes and Twinkies like the other kids."

"I know that," Magda says. "Don't you think I know that? You didn't want anything. A Barbie doll, and new clothes, but nothing in the way of mothering. Reading to you or anything like that. I could march around freeing South Africa or saving Glen Canyon but I couldn't do one thing for my own

37

child."

They are both quiet for a minute. On TV, a woman in an airport knits a longer and longer sweater, apparently unable to stop, while her plane is delayed again and again.

"I know you didn't want to be taken care of, honey," Magda says. "But I guess I just couldn't help it."

Annemarie turns her head to the side, ponderously, as if it has become an enormous egg. She'd forgotten and now remembers how pain seems to increase the size of things. "You know what's crazy?" she asks. "Now I want to be taken care of and nobody will. Men, I mean."

"They would if you'd let them. You act like you don't deserve any better."

"That's not true." Annemarie is surprised and a little resentful at Magda's analysis.

"It *is* true. You'll take a silk blouse from a complete stranger, but not the least little thing from anybody that loves you. Not even a bottle of shampoo. If it comes from somebody that cares about you, you act like it's not worth having."

"Well, you're a good one to talk."

"What do you mean?" Magda pushes the tray table back and turns toward her daughter, carefully, resting her chin on her hand.

"What I mean is you beat men off with a stick. Bartholomew thinks you're Miss America and you don't want him around you. You don't even miss Daddy."

Magda stares at Annemarie. "You don't know the first thing about it. Where were you when he was dying? Outside playing hopscotch."

That is true. That's exactly where Annemarie was.

"Do you remember that upholstered armchair we had, Annemarie, with the grandfather clocks on it? He sat in that chair, morning till night, with his lungs filling up. Worrying about us. He'd say, 'You won't forget to lock the doors, will you? Let's write a little note and tape it there by the door.'

And I'd do it. And then he'd say, 'You know that the brakes on the car have to be checked every so often. They loosen up. And the oil will need to be changed in February.' He sat there looking out the front window and every hour he'd think of another thing, till his face turned gray with the pain, knowing he'd never think of it all."

Annemarie can picture them there in the trailer: two people facing a blank, bright window, waiting for the change that would permanently disconnect them.

Magda looks away from Annemarie. "What hurt him wasn't dying. It was not being able to follow you and me through life looking after us. How could I ever give anybody that kind of grief again?"

The woman who just had the twins has turned off her program, and Annemarie realizes their voices have gradually risen. She demands in a whisper, "I didn't know it was like that for you when he died. How could I not ever have known that, that it wrecked your life, too?"

Magda looks across Annemarie, out the window, and Annemarie tries to follow her line of vision. There is a parking lot outside, and nothing else to see. A sparse forest of metal poles. The unlit streetlamps stare down at the pavement like blind eyes.

"I don't know," Magda says. "Seems like just how it is with you and me. We're like islands on the moon."

"There's no water on the moon," says Annemarie.

"That's what I mean. A person could walk from one to the other if they just decided to do it."

It's dark. Annemarie is staring out the window when the lights in the parking lot come on all together with a soft blink. From her bed she can only see the tops of the cars glowing quietly in the pink light like some strange crop of luminous mushrooms. Enough time passes, she thinks, and it's tomorrow. Buddy or no Buddy, this baby is going to come. For the first time she lets herself imagine holding a newborn against her stomach, its helplessness and rage pulling on her heart like the greatest tragedy there ever was.

There won't be just one baby, either, but two: her own, and her mother's second daughter. Two more kids with dark, curly hair. Annemarie can see them kneeling in the gravel, their heads identically bent forward on pale, slender necks, driving trucks over the moonlike surface of Island Breezes. Getting trikes for their birthdays, skinning their knees, starting school. Once in a while going down with Magda to the Air Force Base, most likely, to fend off nuclear war.

Magda is still lying on her side, facing Annemarie, but she has drawn the covers up and her eyes are closed. The top of the sheet is bunched into her two hands like a bride's bouquet. The belly beneath pokes forward, begging as the unborn do for attention, some reassurance from the outside world, the flat of a palm. Because she can't help it, Annemarie reaches across and lays a hand on her little sister.

Sassafrass, Cypress & Indigo (an excerpt)

NTOZAKE SHANGE

"Indigo, I don't want to hear another word about it, do you understand me. I'm not setting the table with my Sunday china for fifteen dolls who got their period today!"

"But, Mama, I promised everybody we'd have a party because we were growing up and could be more like women. That's what Sister Mary Louise said. She said that we should feast and celebrate with our very best dresses and our very favorite foods."

"Sister Mary Louise needs to get herself married 'fore she's lost what little of her mind she's got left. I don't want you going round that simple woman's house. You take my good velvet from 'tween those dolls' legs. Go to the store and buy yourself some Kotex. Then you come back here and pack those creatures up. Put them in the attic. Bring yourself back here and I'm going to tell you the truth of what you should be worrying about now you sucha grown woman."

"Mama, I can't do that. I can't put them away. I'll have nobody to talk to. Nobody at all."

"Indigo, you're too big for this nonsense. Do like I say, now."

"Mama. What if I stopped carrying Miranda in the street with me, and left my other friends upstairs all the time, could I leave 'em out then, could I? Please Mama, I know they're dollies. I really do. Sassafrass and Cypress kept all the things they made when they were little, didn't they?"

"That's a lie. Don't you have all their dolls? I can't believe a girl as big as you, wearing a training bra and stockings to school, can't think of nothing but make-believe. But if you promise me that you going to leave them in your room and stop asking me to sing to 'em, feed 'em, and talk with 'em, you can leave them out. Now go on to the store."

Indigo left her lesson book on the kitchen table, went to her mother tearing collards by the sink, and gave her a big hug. Her mother's apron always smelled like cinnamon and garlic no matter how many times it was washed. It smelled of times like this when her mother felt a surge in her bosom like her nipples were exploding with milk again, leaving her damp and sweet, but now it was Indigo's tears that softened her spirit.

"Indigo, you're my littlest baby, but you make it hard for me sometimes, you know that."

"Mama, I can make it easier today 'cause I aweady know what it is you were gonna tell me when I came back from the store."

"You do, do you?"

"Yeah, you were going to tell me that since I became a woman, boys were gonna come round more often, 'cause they could follow the trail of stars that fall from between my legs after dark."

"What?"

"The stars that fall from 'tween my legs can only be seen

by boys who are pure of mind and strong of body."

"Indigo, listen to me very seriously. This is Charleston, South Carolina. Stars don't fall from little colored girls' legs. Little boys don't come chasing after you for nothing good. White men roam these parts with evil in their blood, and every single thought they have about a colored woman is dangerous. You have gotta stop living this make-believe. Please, do that for your mother."

"Every time I tell you something, you tell me about white folks. 'White folks say you can't go here — white folks say you can't do this — you can't do that.' I didn't make up white folks, what they got to do with me? I ain't white. My dolls ain't white. I don't go round bothering white folks!"

"That's right, they come round bothering us, that's what I'm trying to tell you . . ."

"Well if they bothering you so much, you do something about 'em."

"Is that some sass comin' out of your mouth?"

"No, M'am. It's just I don't understand why any ol' white person from outta nowhere would want to hurt us. That's all."

Indigo moved to her mother, with a seriousness about her that left the kitchen emptied of all its fullness and aroma.

"I love you so much, Mama. & you are a grown colored woman. Some white man could just come hurt you, any time he wants, too? Oh I could just kill 'em, if they hurt you, Mama. I would. I would just kill anybody who hurt you."

Holding her child as tight as she could, as close into herself as she could, the mother whispered softly as she could, as lovingly as she could, "Well, then we'll both be careful & look after each. Won't we?"

Indigo sort of nodded her head, but all she remembered was that even her mother was scared of white folks, and that she still wrote out the word Kotex on a piece of torn paper wrapped up in a dollar bill to give to Mr. Lucas round to the pharmacy. This, though Indigo insisted Mr. Lucas must know what it is, 'cause he ordered it for his store so all the other colored women could have it when they needed it. After all, even her mother said, this bleeding comes without fail to every good girl once a month. Sometimes her mother made no sense at all, Indigo thought with great consternation. On the other hand, as a gesture of goodwill & in hopes that her littlest girl would heed her warnings, the mother allowed Indigo one more public jaunt with Miranda, who was, according to Indigo, fraught with grief that their outings were to be curtailed.

Weeping willows curled up from the earth, reaching over Indigo & Miranda on this their last walk in a long friendship, a simple, laughing friendship. Miranda thought the weeping willows were trying to hug them, to pull them up to the skies where whether you were real or not didn't matter. Indigo, in her most grown-up voice, said, "No, they want us to feel real special on this day, that's all." Miranda wasn't convinced, and neither was Indigo, who managed to take the longest walk to the drugstore that her family had ever known.

Ending
(an excerpt)

HILMA WOLITZER

The postcard was printed:

Dear Mrs. (and here my name had been typed in). It is now six months since your last gynecological checkup. An appointment has been arranged for you on Thursday, January 23rd, at 10 a.m. If for some reason you cannot keep this appointment, please notify this office at least 48 hours before the scheduled time.

The same postcards always came twice a year to my mother and me. We arrange to have our appointments on the same day and in the past we had gone shopping together and out for lunch. I called my mother and told her that I didn't think I was up to it now, that I would go at some other time. (Thinking — never again, what difference does it make, who cares.) We hung up and a few minutes later she called back and gave me a long lecture about taking care of myself for the sake of the children, that I owed it to Jay to be both mother and father to them, that my body was a sacred temple, that she hated to go by herself — sometimes she felt a little dizzy afterwards, you read in the paper about not waiting too long, because God knows what's going on inside you, God forbid, and I couldn't stop living, even if I felt like it.

Finally I said, "All right, all right," and she breathed a long whistling sigh. "Tootsie," she said. "I know how you feel."

We traveled together as we always did. I drove to the beauty shop and honked the horn two times.

My father came out with a hairbrush in his hand. Inscribed on his smock in an intricate scrolled script was *Mr. B*. He reached in the window and touched my cheek and I saw that his hand trembled slightly. "She'll be out in a minute," he said. "She's just getting her coat."

"Go inside, Daddy. It's cold."

"I'm all right," he insisted. "I can take the cold." But he backed away anyway, waving, and went into the store. Then in a few minutes they appeared together at the doorway and my father reached into his pocket for his wallet. He gestured briefly toward the car and then he gave her some money.

My mother ran in those funny choppy steps, as if her legs were tied together, and then she sat down beside me in the car. "We shouldn't have had a Thursday," she said. "It's a busy day for us. They should have given us a Monday or a Tuesday."

"Ma," I said. "I was willing to change."

"Tootsie, some things can't be put off." She lowered the visor mirror to look at herself, leaning close and squinting. She lifted her lips in a terrible leer and shook her head. "Don't neglect your teeth," she said.

At the clinic we went into adjoining curtained booths and undressed. We put on the paper gowns and slippers provided for us and then we opened the curtains and sat on the little stools and waited.

A nurse came by and said that they were a little delayed and that we would have to wait about fifteen minutes. "So just relax," she advised.

"Ha!" my mother said. Then she reached behind her and brought her pocketbook onto her lap. "I want to give you something."

"Ma," I said. "We have medical insurance. The network has been very generous."

"Take it for Daddy. He specifically said."

The paper gowns rustled as I held out my hand. "Tell him thank you. Thank you both."

"I always hate this," she said, looking around.

"Waiting?"

"The whole business. I know they don't even think about us, the doctors. Not as women. But it makes me nervous, anyway, to put my feet up like that." She shuddered.

"It only takes a few minutes." In my head I lie on the bed at home, my arms opened. Oh come into me. Your voice enters me. Come in. Jay parts my legs like brambles in a forest and goes through.

"Yeah, well . . ." my mother said.

"Think about something else. Pretend you're in Paris and Doctor Miller is your lover."

"Some lover."

"Pretend you're at the dentist's. Open wide now, dear."

"You!" She blushed. "Listen, do you know what I do. I shut my mind off completely."

"I wish that I could do that."

"I thought you didn't mind the examination."

"Not that," I said. "I just wish that I didn't have to think."

"My poor girl," she said, and she patted my hand. She looked down at her bare legs, embroidered with blue veins. "Older people should go first."

"No," I said. "Nobody should go, ever."

"Don't be crazy. It would be like the BMT in the rush

47

hour. As you get older, you change, anyway." She stood up and stepped back into her booth. She crooked her finger. "Come here for a second."

I walked into her booth and she reached up and pulled the curtain. Then she parted the gown and lifted it. "I once had a beautiful figure," she said. "Look at that."

Her skin was mottled pink and white, as if she had just come from a hot bath. Her breasts were two pale tilting moons. There were sharp red marks where her girdle had held her and the thin line of an old scar ran across her belly, disappearing into the sparse, graying bush. She pointed to the trembling flesh of her thigh.

"Ma," I said, "you still . . ."

"Feel that. Just feel that."

I reached out and touched her skin briefly.

She smiled triumphantly. "*That's* what happens!" She lowered the gown and opened the curtain again.

I went back to my own booth and sat down.

"It happens to everyone," she said. "Things don't work so well anymore."

"Don't you feel well? Is it Daddy?"

She shrugged. "*Everybody* slows down. You can't do all the things you could *always* do."

Suddenly I realized what she was talking about. I leaned over to look at her and she was staring down into the open pocketbook in her lap. I wanted to say something compassionate, as if she had just told me of the sudden death of a friend, but I found that I couldn't speak.

"*Some* people think that they are going to live forever, that time is never going to get in their way." Her mouth closed in a narrow furrow.

I wanted to say, "Forgive him then." I felt terribly disloyal, knowing this news of my father. I thought of him looking at his own reflection above the head of a seated customer, combing his moustache, sucking in his belly and then letting it out again with a long hissing sigh. I imagined that she thought he had met a just punishment. I wanted to say, "Forgive him," but my mother snapped her pocketbook shut with a final click that ended the conversation.

Then the nurse came down the hall, humming a tune. "Okay, girls," she said. "You're on."

Complex

BINNIE KIRSHENBAUM

This shopping mall has a name. The Gallery, it's called. If it were up to me, instead of attempting to personalize a clone, I would ride the wave of the future and number the shopping malls: Mall #1, Mall #2, Mall #378, because shopping malls are very postmodern. I've been to shopping malls in Buffalo, New Haven, Denver, Brooklyn and Cleveland and sure enough, each time there was the Florsheim Shoes on the lower level left, Walden Books across the way and Baskin-Robbins in the far right corner. I suspect too much time spent in shopping malls could result in a waking nightmare but this is only my sixth visit to one. I'm here, in this one, with Alma, my mother.

"Incredible, Alma," I say. "Look, there's the fountain exactly where it's supposed to be. And the Photo-Mat right off the escalator. It's déjà vu."

Alma's crazy for a shopping mall too. "All your shopping under one roof. It is so convenient," she says.

"They're art, you know," I say. "These malls. The suburban statement." But Alma, whose ideas about art range from Norman Rockwell to Andrew Wyeth, isn't following me. "Is Burger King art too?" she asks.

Alma and I are having this outing because Alma's friend Helen plays tennis with *her* daughter every day. "And I never see *my* daughter," is the way Alma put it to me. "Helen and *her* daughter are such good friends. I always thought we'd be good friends."

When Alma gets on that kick, there is no point to giving her the facts. "So go ahead," I said, "reserve a court for us."

Alma knows as well as I do that we would look hideous playing tennis. "There's no need to be sarcastic like that," Alma said. "But you could come up one Saturday. We could go to the Gallery and have lunch."

Alma, pacing the platform, pounced on me when I got off the train. "I was worried about you," she said. "You told me you were getting in at ten o'clock. I was here at a quarter of. The train pulled in at ten sharp and you weren't on it. I got nervous."

"I told you, Alma," I said, "I was *taking* the ten o'clock train. Which would get me here at ten forty."

"Oh," said Alma, deflating like a runaway balloon.

I reminded Alma of when I was a kid dizzy with the prospect of Lori Kessel's birthday party. "Remember how I dressed myself in my party frock, tucked the present under my arm and rapped at the Kessels' door with my sweaty little fists? I was so mortified when Mrs. Kessel told me I'd arrived a day too early."

Alma opened the car door and said, "I just misunderstood, that's all."

I slid into the passenger's seat. Alma instructed me to buckle up. She turned the ignition key but left the car in idle. Twisting my direction and preparing her words as if she had some gruesome news to give me, Alma said, "Um . . . your hair . . . it's messed . . . funny." I pulled the rearview mirror my way and took a look. "It's supposed to be like that," I said.

The parking lot adjacent to the Gallery is nearly as spectacular as the mall itself. Yet another wonder of the world; four mind-boggling levels of concrete slab and row upon row of family-style cars parked with the uniformity of gravestones at Arlington.

I questioned how we'd ever find our car again. I got a vision of standing in the lot until well past dinner time waiting for everyone else to drive away, locating Alma's Volvo by virtue of its being the only car left. "Does that ever happen?" I asked Alma.

"The parking lot is coded," she said. "We're on the third level, aisle G, spot 27."

"What a concept," I said and Alma asked, "Whatever are you talking about?"

I want to look at the hokey stuff, stores like Ye Olde Gift Shoppe or that one which sells brass decorative items — for the same reasons I watch game shows on TV, but Alma wants to look at clothes. In the boutiques. "They have some darling shops here," Alma says.

"Darling, huh?" I say.

A lot of mall dwellers are staring at me. Not the same way they'd stare at dwarves or cripples but more get-a-load-of-that look. Alma and I approach a gaggle of girls who are a few years younger than me. This, hanging out at the mall, is no doubt their raison d'etre. Sporting last year's haircuts, these voidoids are stuffed into watered-down versions, really, of what I wear, but so diluted as to not be recognizable as such. Two of them actually have on sweatshirts cropped by the manufacturer. As I pass, they elbow each other and snicker. Alma spots me turning back to give these twinkies a scowl and says, "Don't they look cute? I like their style."

And I say, "Style? What style? They don't have any style."

Alma tells me I ought not to be so critical. "They probably don't like the way you look either."

None of the stores in the Gallery have doors, which is part of the beauty of a mall. It's a wilderness of shopping. Not missing a beat, we are in Jean's Closet. From the looks of things, I'd say this is pretty much where that gang out there with the frosted nail polish shops. Still, I take inventory. Maybe something will grab me because it's a sure bet Alma will spring for a new blouse or skirt if I find something I like. However, that appears doubtful. Jean's Closet features the same colors the Baskin-Robbins does: strawberry pinks, pistachio greens, cherry-vanilla and lemon.

From across the store Alma calls out for me. That used to make me want to shrivel up and die, my mother calling my name in a store. I used to be terrified someone I knew would be there to hear and know I was with my mother, of all creatures. It doesn't humiliate me like it used to, though. That was a very difficult period for Alma, the one when I tried to pretend I didn't have a mother.

Before she can shout for me again, I zigzag across the aisles over to her. She is holding up a pleated skirt, navy blue and Greenwich Connecticut green. It comes with a matching scarf and hat which resembles the one Sherlock Holmes wore. Alma adores outfits. And sets. Everything she buys me has at least two parts: a paisley scarf that came with a paisley address book, a beige umbrella with brown trim and a contrasting tote, a seed pearl necklace which was not complete without the seed pearl bracelet and brooch. Once she got me a chintz blouse that was packaged with a pair of earrings made from the same fabric. "Wherever did you find that?" I'd asked.

"Isn't it the loveliest set?" Alma answered.

Alma has bought me eyeglass cases that go with wallets and cosmetic bags, pocketbook and matching handkerchief sets, tissue boxes that have companion garbage cans and a pen and pencil duo with coordinating notebook and calculator.

Now, Alma is interested in this three-piece plaid affair. "Try it on," she says. "Humor me. Come on."

Alma leads the way into the dressing room. She prepares the outfit, taking it off the hanger, while I step out of my things. "You know this has a hole in it," Alma says about my dress as she takes it in exchange.

I burst out laughing as I look at myself in the mirror. Alma adjusts the scarf. "There," she says, "like so." I look like an insane person in this number, plaid scarf dipping around my black lace bra. "The aftermath of a lobotomy," I say, but Alma thinks otherwise. "Of course," she says, "it needs a blouse. But otherwise, you look smashing. Like you belong on the cover of *Seventeen*."

My mother wants to buy me this get-up. I tell her I'd rather have the cash. Alma looks so disappointed. I tell her it's really a keen outfit but I wouldn't have any occasion to wear something like that. "But it's so practical," Alma says. "You're sure you don't want it?"

I pluck the hat off and pass it to Alma. It's flattened my spikes, that goofy hat. I run my fingers through my hair trying to get it to stand up again.

Like two ghosts passing through a plate of glass, Alma and I glide into WaldenBooks. Alma pauses to look at more than just titles. She flips through a couple of books with pictures. "This place," I say to Alma, "is like a Roumanian bookstore, don't you think?" The joke is lost on my mother. The last time Alma voted was in 1960, right before I was born. She voted for John Kennedy because, "He was so handsome. And Daddy voted for him." In this vein, not long ago, Alma mentioned to me she'd watched a news broadcast airing from

Ethiopia. Her TV screen filled up with famine victims. "Why did they show that on the news?" Alma asked me. "It was a horrible thing to have to look at."

"You know," I try to explain to her, "this is a bookstore but it is spare on real books. All they sell here is propaganda." Alma looks at me blankly and I ask, "Alma, do you even know where Roumania is?"

Ignoring the question, Alma tells me about a novel she is reading. She tells me the title. It is a novel I have heard about. It's one of those fat ones; a lot of pages.

"It's on the *New York Times* bestseller list," Alma says.

"I know," I say.

"It's a wonderful story," says Alma. "I'll loan it to you when I'm done."

I tell her not to bother. "It's not the sort of book I care to read."

"But it's a bestseller," Alma says.

"Alma, that does not make it a good book," I say.

"Must you be so contrary?" Alma asks. I think she is still hurt over my not wanting the plaid clown suit.

Planted on the checkout counter at WaldenBooks is a two-foot-high cardboard tree. Clinging to it are Fuzzies. Fuzzies are these little furry bears and cats and geegaws whose arms clip to pens and notebooks. There is a sign in front of the tree which reads: GIVE A FUZZIE TO A FRIEND TODAY. Alma buys two of them. Outside of the bookstore, she gives me the bear. I wonder who the geegaw is for.

Alma asks if I mind spending a few minutes with her while she looks for a lamp. Light Up Your Life is three shops down from the WaldenBooks. Alma tells me she is looking for a lamp for the den. "A desk lamp," she says. The den used to be my bedroom. Alma and my father took it over after I left, which was fine by me although Alma thought it necessary to ask my permission. "You understand it doesn't mean anything," Alma had said. "You can still come back anytime you want. It will always be your room."

"I'm not coming back, Alma," I say. "Do anything you want with my bedroom. Take in a boarder, if you want."

My friend Mah-Jong told me her mother has kept her bedroom exactly as she left it ten years ago. "It's a shrine to a pom-pom girl," Mah-Jong told me. Mah-Jong has the solar system tattooed on her back. "It's creepy," she said. "Like stepping into the Twilight Zone. Decaying stuffed animals, collecting dust, stare down from their perch-like icons. An 8x10 glossy of my high school graduation picture in a pink frame lurks on the nightstand. You wouldn't even recognize me in that picture," Mah-Jong said. "I had brown hair then. And eyebrows. If you can believe that. It's a sick place, that bedroom. It's waiting for me to come home to die."

Alma was bothered that I had no feelings concerning my bedroom being turned into a den. That's how Alma is. First, she's worried I'll get upset and then she's peeved when I don't.

I never liked that bedroom anyway. To me, it looked like a Lily Pulitzer dress. Pinks and greens and lavenders. With lace trim. Those colors were assaulting me. To me, entering my bedroom was like opening one of those laughing boxes you get in novelty stores. I used to plead with Alma to let me paint my bedroom walls black. "In your own apartment," Alma had said, "you can have black walls. But not in my house, you don't."

Alma can't find the lamp she is after. Alma is fussy about details like a lamp. Alma prides herself on the way she fixes a room up. She has what she calls a flair for decorating. Often, she refers to herself as creative. She has done the den in browns and forest greens. The furniture is oak. It doesn't look anything like the way I'd do a den. I'd do it in whites. Stark whites with a fake fur polar bear rug in front of a white plexiglass drafting table. Instead of the country road in autumn painting Alma's got hanging, I'd put up a Larry Rivers. If I fixed a place up, that is. Right now, that's not a priority with me. When I first got my apartment, Alma had plans for it. She approached me with fabric swatches and said, "I'd love to help you decorate."

"Decorate? I'm only going to put in a bookshelf, Alma. You know, the necessities."

"I always thought it was something we'd do together," Alma said, "fix up your first apartment." She put the swatches back in her purse.

"Oh Alma," I put my arm around her. "Where do you get such ideas?"

Alma and I get separated on the escalator. I thought she was right behind me. Instead I find my mother at the Thom McCann's admiring baby shoes. "Come along," I take Alma by the arm, "this isn't good for you."

We stroll along the waxed promenade, window shopping, until I tell Alma I am hungry. "Famished," I say. "Ravenous."

Alma wants to take me to Taters. Taters is her favorite place to dine at the Gallery. "Sort of the hot spot, is it?" I ask.

"Don't make fun," Alma says.

Taters is on the lookout point of the mall. From our seats, we have an aerial view of the place. "It's like Windows on the World," I say. I scout over the balcony for people I know. Or rather, people I knew. Maybe someone I went to high school with, someone I would not want to see at all except maybe for a goof, is shopping here today.

The menu at Taters is baked potatoes which are split open and stuffed with things. They give you a choice of seventy-six different things to glop into these potatoes: cheese, vegetables, chili, marshmallows. Alma is under the notion that this is health food. "I usually get the asparagus with cheddar cheese," she says. Alma is proud.

I order a baked potato stuffed with hot-dog bits and Boston beans. "This place is so wild," I say. "Really," I add because Alma does not know what to make of me sometimes.

"It's such a superb idea. Ahead of itself. Did you know, Alma, that YooHoo has made a comeback? But these," I make a sweep over our potatoes, "these are social commentary. I am going to serve stuffed baked potatoes the next time I have a dinner party. It's sure to be a rage."

"You give dinner parties?" Alma asks. "I didn't know you ever gave dinner parties. I've never even been to your apartment." This is true. When Alma comes into the city to see me, I meet her at Grand Central Station. Or in front of Bloomingdale's. "It's for your own safety, Alma," I say. "Honest. You don't want to see where I live. You really don't."

Alma is offended, I recognize the symptoms by now. I offend Alma frequently. I don't mean to offend her. It just works out that way.

Alma surfaces with a brave smile and wants to know if I'm still going with that boy I brought home a few months ago. At first, my parents were put off by Spark's appearance. "He wears earrings," my father said. And Alma asked, carefully, if he'd recently had surgery. "Why then," she wanted to know, "is his head shaved in spots like that?" But Spark has got a way of getting people to take to him. By the end of dinner he was calling Alma "Mom" and helping her with the dishes. She said he had very nice manners. Even my father said, "Pleasant enough young man."

To demonstrate how hip they can be and also how they thought well of Spark, Alma and my father didn't say boo over Spark and I sleeping together in the guest room. "Your parents are pretty cool," Spark said to me. "I mean, I've met worse."

"Do you think you'll marry him?" Alma asks. I've never told Alma about Spark's affection for handcuffs.

"Marry Spark? No. I wouldn't marry Spark."

"But you're going with him." Alma means this ought to lead to something.

I know where this conversation is headed. No place I'm interested in. So I change the subject and I tell Alma about the new band I'm managing. "They're cool, Alma. They don't play instruments but they play tools. Electric tools. Drills and jack hammers and buzz saws."

"A modern washboard band," says Alma.

"A what?" I ask and Alma says never mind.

"It's a totally new concept," I say. "And a neat sound. You know, it's not exactly music as we know it. It's more of a performance, really."

"And people come to hear them play?" Alma asks.

"Well," I tell her, "they don't exactly play. But they will. Soon. You see, that's where I come in. I'm their PR person. Public relations. Hype them up. And I book them into clubs. For now, they're doing freebies. Just to get heard. Once they get enough exposure, they're bound to take off. It's practically a sure thing."

Alma wants to know what I'm getting for my efforts and so I explain to her about how I get to hang out with the musicians and go to the clubs for free.

"But no one pays to hear them anyway," says Alma. "So you could do all that without the running around."

I tell Alma that she just doesn't understand and she says, "No. I guess I don't."

I must be psychic. Again I can see what's coming next. Only I can't think how to duck this one. I know that look on Alma's face, the one where her lips get so narrow, they invert. Alma has got ideas for me which have got to do with some other daughter. One she didn't have. "I worry," Alma says on cue. "I can't help it but I worry. You have no security. What will become of you?" Alma wants me to get a job with benefits.

I try to explain to Alma that I don't want my life to be a piece of the rock. "I don't want what you have, Alma," I say. "I hated it here, you know. This town. This lifestyle. It was all wrong for me. I was unhappy here. I never fit in."

"And whose fault was that?" Alma wants to know.

We poke at the remains of our stuffed potatoes. We're making a mess of our outing, it seems. Except Alma can be counted on to salvage the remains. "Let's talk about other things," she says. "Something pleasant."

"Okay," I say and ask for gossip. I adore gossip.

"Do you remember Carol Donohue?" Alma asks. "She committed suicide. She's a Catholic, you know. Andrea Gallager told me they don't say Mass for her. No one was invited to the funeral or even knows where she's buried. The Church wouldn't have her." Alma takes a sip of coffee.

This is better gossip than I'd hoped for. I am eager for the details and ask a flood of questions, but Alma only shrugs and says, "Who knows. Why would a person kill themselves? I have no idea. She seemed to have everything a woman could want." Alma wants to move on to another topic. She doesn't like it that I'm interested in Mrs. Donohue's suicide. "Let's see," Alma says. "What else? Oh, guess who got married? Maxine Chamblay. Someone finally married the poor dear. She's almost thirty, you know."

"Thirty does not exactly qualify a girl for spinsterdom, Alma."

"Oh, I know that. It's just that she had those dreadful teeth."

Maxine Chamblay's teeth gnarled and intertwined, resembling a pair of arthritic hands. Plus she had two extra teeth, eye teeth, growing down from the roof of her mouth like a pair of stalactites. I used to give her quarters to let me touch them. Alma was always saying, "Why don't they get that poor dear to an orthodontist?" I wonder if this boy Maxine has married runs his tongue along her snaggleteeth?

Alma asks if I want more coffee. "Sure," I say. "I'm in no hurry."

"You'll stay for dinner, won't you?" Alma wants to

know. "Your father hasn't seen you in ages. And I bought your favorite. Pork chops."

Pork chops are not my favorite. I suspect they are Alma's favorite. She wants desperately for us to have something in common. As pork chops don't make me retch or give me hives, I don't tell Alma that pork chops are not on the top of my chart.

"Sure. I'll stay for dinner," I say. "I don't have to be back in the city until ten or so. There's this new band I want to go hear tonight. Rumor has it they're looking for a manager. They're reputed to be fab. They could go places."

"What do they play?" Alma asks. "A ten-speed blender and an electric range?" Alma likes her little joke. So do I, only I think it's got possibilities.

"Alma, you may be on to something." I think out loud, putting together a girl group. Beehive hair-do's. They'll wear aprons, those 1950s aprons, over spandex. And mules on their feet. And they'll play modern kitchen implements. Cuisinarts, electric knives, mix-masters. "It's a statement. Betty Crocker and the Brownies. No. Too obvious. Let's see. Cheesecake. That's it. Cheesecake."

"You're not serious," Alma says.

I tell her I am quite serious. "It's a sensational idea. Do you mind if I use it? I mean, it was yours but I can have it, can't I?"

"But it was just a joke," Alma says.

"Maybe to you it was just a joke. But I think this could go places."

"I worry about you," Alma says.

"Don't worry about me, Alma."

I tell Alma I have to go to the bathroom. She starts to give me directions but I wave them off. "I know. Second floor. Far right corner. Just off India Imports, right?"

"Yes," says Alma.

"You know, Alma, there's an elegance to monolithism."

61

I take an extra minute in the bathroom trying to get my hair to stand up again. I think that plaid hat did permanent damage, as if just trying it on took some of the bite out of my method.

There is a blouse in the window of India Imports which isn't too grotesque. I could do things with it. And it is black, at least. I'll go get Alma over here to buy it for me. She hates when I go home empty-handed.

I come back to our booth at Taters to find Alma leafing through one of her photo-wallets. Alma's got several of them, the vinyl sort usually associated with grandparents who whip out yardage of pictures of their grandchildren to bore strangers with. Alma also has an infinite number of photo-albums. Alma likes to hold on to what she perceives as precious moments. She is always one for grabbing the camera and saying, "Please. For me. I don't have any pictures of you." This is, of course, pure myth. Alma has got mountains of pictures of me. Pictures of me with Santa Claus at Macy's, pictures of me taking pony rides at the zoo. Pictures of the first and last days of school from kindergarten through college. She's got snaps of me going on my first date and one of me taking my first leak successfully on the toilet. And still, she wants more. All the time she says, "Smile. For me." Alma's got my history on Kodak color.

I lean across the table. She's got the wallet open to one of me standing on the front lawn. I'm a lot smaller and chunkier. I must be only three or four in that picture. But even from this position, upside-down, that's my face all right. I'm wearing a blue and white polka-dot pinafore and am carrying a matching parasol. "Hey," I say, "I remember that outfit. I thought it was the snazziest thing going."

But Alma is not listening to me. She is flipping through her card catalogue of what was and what could have been.

I lean back into the yellow plastic booth and think of dying my hair aubergine. That's a kind of purple.

A Touch
of the Flu

JOYCE CAROL OATES

For years she tried to conceive a child, and failed; and failed at the marriage too — though "failed" is probably the wrong word, since, wanting a child so badly, and, as some observers (including her husband) said, so irrationally, she simply decided to give up on that man, and move on to another. And so she did; and conceived within months; and had her baby, a little girl; and lived with her alone, since, by that time, she'd come to understand that there was no room in her life for both the baby and the baby's father. Even had he wanted to marry her, which was not so clearly the case.

And she was happy with her little girl, if not, as she'd anticipated, ecstatic; except of course in bursts of feeling; wayward, unexpected, dazzling, and brief. These are the moments for which we live, she thought. She wondered if anyone had had that thought before her.

That summer she brought her daughter to Maine, to her parents' summer home, and there, each morning, pushed her in a stroller along the beach. She sang to her litle girl, talked to her almost continuously, for there was no one in the world except the two of them, and, by way of the two of them, their delicious union, the world became new, newly created. She held her little girl in her arms, aloft, in triumph, her heart swelling with love, exaltation, greed. Sand, ocean, butterfly, cloud, sky, do you see? Wind, sun, — do you feel?

But one day she was overcome by a sensation of lightheadedness, and exhaustion, and returned to the house after only a few minutes on the beach, and handed the baby over to her mother, and went to bed; and did not get up for ten days; during which time she did not sleep, nor was she fully awake; simply lying in bed, in her old girlhood bed, her eyes closed, or, if open, staring at the ceiling, sightless and unjudging. Her mother brought her little girl to nurse, and she pushed her away, in revulsion, and could not explain; for it was herself she saw, in her mother's arms, as it had been, so suddenly, herself she'd seen, in her little girl, that morning on the beach; and she thought, I cannot bear it. Not again.

Still, the spell lifted, as such spells do. And she got up, and was herself again, or nearly; and nursed her baby again, with as much pleasure as before; or nearly. Her mother looked at her hard and said, "You've had a touch of the flu," and she smiled, and regarded her mother with calm wide intelligent eyes, and said, "Yes, I think that was it. A touch of the flu." And they never spoke of it again.

The Proposal

KIM CHERNIN

July 1974 **S**he calls me on the telephone three times the day before I am due to arrive in Los Angeles. The first time she says, "Tell me, you still like cottage cheese?" "Sure," I say, "I love it. Cottage cheese, yogurt, ricotta . . ." "Good," she says, "we'll have plenty."

The second conversation is much like the first. "What about chicken? You remember how I used to bake it?"

The third time she calls the issue is schav — Russian sorrel soup, served cold, with sour cream, chopped egg, and onion, large chunks of dry black bread. "Mama," I say. "Don't worry. It's you I'm coming to visit. It doesn't matter what we eat."

She worries. She is afraid she has not been a good mother. An activist when I was growing up, Communist Party organizer, she would put up our dinner in a huge iron pot before she left for work each morning, in this way making sure she neglected no essential duty of a mother and wife. For this, however, she had to get up early. I would watch her, chopping onions and tomatoes, cutting a chicken up small, dicing meat, while I ate breakfast, sitting on a small stepladder at our chopping board.

Now, thirty years later, she's afraid she won't be able to give whatever it is I come looking for when I come for a visit. I'm laughing, and telling my daughter about her three calls, and I am weeping.

"What's schav?" my daughter asks me as we get off the plane in Los Angeles. "There's Grandma," I say, "ask her," as I wave to my mother, trying to suggest some topic of conversation for this eleven-year-old American girl and the woman in her seventies who was born in a small Jewish village in Russia.

My mother catches sight of us and immediately begins talking in an excited voice over the heads of people in line before us as we come through the disembarkation lane. I love this about her, this extravagance of feeling, the moodiness that goes along with it.

"Mama," I call out, waving excitedly, while my daughter looks at her feet and falls back with embarrassment as I push forward into my mother's arms.

She takes me by the elbow as we make our way toward the baggage, giving me sideways her most cunning look. What does she see? I look at myself with her eyes. Suddenly, I'm a giant. Five feet, four and a half inches tall the last time I measured myself, now I'm strolling along here as if I'm on stilts. She has to tip back her head to look into my eyes. This woman, whose hands were once large enough to hold my entire body, does not now reach as high as my daughter's shoulder.

We are all trying to think of something to say. We hurry past murals on the terminal walls. Finally, it is my mother who speaks. "Who are you running from?" she says, tugging me by the arm. "Let me get a look at you."

She stops and looks into my eyes. Then she looks at Larissa. Deeply perceptive, this look of hers. Assessing. Eyes narrowing. "A beauty," she whispers to me as Larissa goes off to stand near the baggage chute. But then she straightens her back and tilts her head up. "It's good you came now," she whispers. "It's important."

She comes up close to me, her shoulder resting against mine. "There's something I didn't tell you."

"You don't have to tell me," I say as quietly as possible. "I already know."

"You know?" She looks doubtful, but only for a moment. "Hoie," she sighs, "you were always like this. Who can keep anything from you?"

"Is she in pain?"

"Pain, sorrow, who can distinguish? There is, let me tell you, a story here. If you would write it down in a book, nobody would believe you."

I know better than to ask about the story. In my family they hint and retreat and tell you later in their own good time.

"But this is not for now," she says, turning her head sharply. "She won't last long, that much I know."

"What do the doctors say?"

"I should wait for doctors to tell me about my own sister?" Her voice has an edge to it, an impatience. But I know her by now. With this tone she attempts to master her own pain.

I want to put my arms around her, to comfort her for the loss of Aunt Gertrude. But I'm afraid she'll push me away, needing her own strength more than she needs my comfort.

"You know doctors," she continues, softening. "For every one thing they tell you, there are two things hidden under the tongue."

"And you?" I ask, because it seems to me she'll let the question come now. "How are you?"

She gestures dismissively with her hand and I know what will follow. *"Gezunt vi gezunt,"* she snorts, with her grim, shtetl humor: "Never mind my health, just tell me where to get potatoes."

Larissa waves. She has been making faces at me, as if the luggage is much too heavy for her to carry; she drags it along, wiping her forehead with an imaginary rag.

"What's this?" my mother calls out. "We leave the child to carry the luggage?"

But I am wringing my hands. I have put my fists against my temples, rocking myself with exaggerated woe. My mother looks at me, frowning, puzzled. There is a playfulness between Larissa and me, a comradeship she does not understand. When I was pregnant with Larissa I used to dream about running with her through the park, a small child at play with a larger one called the mother.

But now my mother cries out, "Wait, wait, we'll help you, don't strain like this."

She is confused by our sudden bursts of wildness; she frowns and seems to be struggling to understand the meaning of playfulness.

"It's a joke, Mama," I have to tell her, "a game we play."

Then, with hesitation, she smiles. But it is here I see most clearly the difference in our generations. Hers, with its eye fixed steadily on survival. Mine freer, more frivolous, less scarred and, in my own eyes, far less noble.

Now she has understood what Larissa is doing.

"Another one, look at her," she calls out, shaking her hands next to her head, leaning forward. "Both crazy."

We take up the suitcases and walk out toward the car. Larissa is carrying the two small duffel bags that make it clear we have come for only a few days.

But my mother has not overlooked this symbolism. And now, refusing my hand when I reach out for her, she says, "Three and a half years you haven't been to visit. You think you're living in the North Pole?"

"Berkeley, the North Pole, what's the difference?" I say,

irresistibly drawn into her idiom. "It would take a team of huskies to drag me away from my work."

"Your work," she says, with all the mixed pride and ambivalence she feels about the fact that I live alone with my daughter, supporting both of us as a private teacher, involved in a work of solitary scholarship and poetry she does not understand.

"Still the same thing?" she asks, a tone of uncertainty creeping into her voice. "Mat-ri-archy?"

Reluctantly, I nod my head. But it is not like us to avoid a confrontation. "Tell me," she says, in a hushed, conspiratorial tone, as if she were making an alliance with my better nature. "Tell me, this is serious work you are doing?"

Once, years ago, coming down to visit I grew so angry that when we reached home I called a taxi and returned to the airport again.

"Mama," I say, my voice already too vehement, "listen to me." Larissa falls back and walks beside me. "In doing this work I am breaking taboos as great as those you broke when you became a Communist."

I know that my daughter wants me to lower my voice. Her face is puckered and worried. I put my hand on her shoulder, changing my tone.

"Believe me, where women are concerned, there are still ideas it is as difficult to think as it was once difficult for Marx to understand the fact that bourgeoise society was built upon the exploitation of the workers."

Since I was a small girl I have been fighting with my mother. When the family was eating dinner some petty disagreement would arise and I'd jump up from the table, pick up a plate and smash it against the wall. I'd go running from the room, slamming doors behind me.

By the age of thirteen I insisted that Hegel was right and not Marx. "The Idea came first," I cried out from the bathroom, which had the only door in the house that locked. "The

Spirit came before material existence."

In the afternoons I read books. I started on the left side of the bookcase, at the top shelf, and thumbed my way through every book in the library. *The Classics of Marxism, Scottsboro Boy, State and Revolution* by Lenin, a story about the Huck Bella Hop in the Philippines, stories about the Spanish civil war.

I understood little of what I read, but I built a vocabulary, a mighty arsenal of weapons to use against my mother.

Then, when she came into the house, I was ready for her. Any opinion she uttered, I took the opposite point of view. If she liked realism, I preferred abstract art. If she believed in internationalism, I spoke about the necessity to concentrate on local conditions.

Twenty years later nothing has changed. We still refuse to understand one another, both of us still protesting the fact we are so little alike.

Her voice rises; she has clenched her jaw. "You're going to tell me about the exploitation of the workers?"

I answered belligerently, shaking with passion. "There is the same defiance of authority in the scholarship I do, the same passion for truth in the poetry I write as there has been in your life."

"Truth? We're going to discuss truth now?"

"And it changes, doesn't it? From generation to generation?"

The silence that follows this outburst is filled up through every cubic inch of itself by my shame. We are not even out of the airport and already I've lost my temper. And this time especially I had wanted so much to draw close to her. Surely, it must be possible after all these years.

"Mama," I say, throwing my arm around her shoulders with the same conspiratorial appeal she has used in approaching me. "You know what I found out? Marx and Engels, both of them, believed there was once a matriarchal stage of social organization. Yes, I'm serious. I'll tell you where you can read it."

"Marx and Engels?" she says. "You don't say. Marx and Engels?"

But now she sighs, shaking her head. "So all right, I am what I am, we can't be the same person. But I don't like to see you spending your life like this, that much I know."

She pauses, looking over at me, and I can see in her eyes the same resolution I have made.

"Let it go, I don't want to quarrel with you. But when I think . . . a woman like you. So brilliant, so well-educated. You could contribute to the world. With your gifts, what couldn't you accomplish?" Then, in her most endearing voice she says, "You're a poet. I accept this. But now I've got something to say to you. And I don't want you to say no before you give it some thought."

I look down at her face, so deeply marked with determination. "Tell me," I say, in spite of myself, for I know she won't tell me now, no matter what I do.

She looks around her. She has always liked a little suspense. She looks over at Larissa, she looks down at our bags. She reaches in her purse and feels around for her keys.

And then finally, taking my arm, she says, confidingly, almost with humor, "So, what's the hurry? We've got time."

At dinner Larissa toys with her food. Who can blame her? From the moment we entered the house my mother has been feeding her. In the first ten minutes she brought out a plate of cookies baked for us by Aunt Sara, my father's brother's wife. Since then, I've seen my mother standing at the kitchen door, her hands at her waist, watching my daughter. "A good eater," she says to no one in particular as Larissa accepts a slice of Jell-O mold. "This is what you used to be like," she adds, turning to me, "before you took it in your head to get so thin."

In the kitchen, lined up on the counter, there are several large platters wrapped in tin foil. They are the gifts brought by my various aunts when they heard I was coming down for a visit. Raisin strudel from Aunt Anne, rolled cinnamon twists from Sara Sol's, a bowl of chopped liver, kugel in an oval pan.

I have always been held in high esteem by my family. "A *chochma,* a wise one," they'd say about me even as a child. "Born with a clear star over her head," his oldest sister would say to my father. "A golden tongue," they'd murmur when I burst out in some extravagant childhood story.

Even to this day, in spite of the fact that I have brought home to them so few tangible signs of worldly fame, they admire me.

They manage to forgive me for my two divorces. They struggle to understand the way I live.

"We never had a poet in the family before," my father's oldest brother said to me before he died. "We're proud of you. If you were born a son, you maybe would have become even a rabbi."

Their family traces itself back to the Vilna Goan, a famous rabbinical scholar of the eighteenth century. But my mother, whenever she heard this, would always snort. "Hach, little people, trying to make themselves feel important."

Her own family was more radical, more violent in its passion, more extreme in its life choices. Each side has always expected me to carry on its tradition. As it is, I have inherited my mother's fierce, revolutionary fervor, my father's quiet inclination for scholarship, and someone else's wild, untutored mystical leanings. They all worry about me because I have become too thin. But the food they have brought me, in love and in tribute, today has been eaten by my daughter.

Larissa moves her food over to the side of her plate, shovels it back toward the center, and makes fork marks in the baked squash.

My mother casts a disapproving glance at her. "Chopped liver she doesn't like. Schav she doesn't like. So eat a mouthful of chicken. Chicken they are eating also among the fifth generation born Americans."

At this, my mother's sister, Aunt Gertrude, who is sitting next to me, throws back her head and emits a dry, conciliatory laugh. It is impossible to recognize in this frail, withdrawn woman, the aunt of my childhood, the woman who joined the Peace Corps at the age of fifty-three, and went off to serve as a nurse in Ethiopia. I have heard that one day she rode a donkey over the mountains, taking supplies to villages of the interior. The image of her has lived on with me, an aging woman with gaunt face and brilliant eyes, her white hair beginning to yellow, the habitual smoker's cough, the clop of the animal's hooves and she rides, talking, smoking, gesturing, over the bad roads of the mountains of Ethiopia.

When I lean close to her I can smell the acrid sweetness I have known since childhood, when my sister was dying. It makes me want to run toward her, to grab her so tight death cannot get hold of her, and it makes me want to run away. I glance toward her from the corner of my eye, knowing she would not like to be stared at. And she, growing conscious of my tact, presses my foot beneath the table.

Her touch is so light I can scarcely feel it, but it has the power to jog my memory. Profoundly moved, I recall the games we used to play together when I was a child visiting at her house, little pokings and pattings, accompanied by puffs from her cigarettes, perfect rings of smoke, the smell of caffeine and the good odor of soap.

She had some secret sorrow, never spoken of, never completely hidden from me. But I knew, even as a small girl, that if you loved this woman you should pretend to believe that she was happy.

"There you be, cookie," she'd say in her husky voice when she came looking for me. I would jump up and throw my arms around her neck, charmed by her gruff tenderness.

She worked hard; she grew old early. "Something's eating her," my mother would say to my father. And I watched the wrinkles gnawing at her face, deepening perceptibly every time I saw her.

Silence comes to our table. Gertrude sipping her black tea, my mother tapping her fork against her plate, my own chair shifting restlessly as it attempts in all futility to establish itself in some permanent niche in the world.

And suddenly I know precisely what my mother has been hinting at since I arrived in Los Angeles. It comes to me from the silence as if it had been clearly and distinctly uttered. Now, in front of my aunt and my daughter, she is going to ask me something impossible to refuse.

She takes a deep breath, looks around the room as if she has misplaced something, and then delivers herself of one of those weighty utterances which have been troubling the atmosphere all day. "Do you know why I'm alive today?" she says, as if it were a question of her own will that she has lived to be an old woman. "Do you want to know why I'm still living?" And then, when Larissa looks toward her expectantly: "Because," she says, "there's still injustice in the world. And I am a fighter."

My mother's conversation frequently assumes this rhetorical tone. It comes, I suppose, from the many years she has been a public speaker. Even her English changes at such moments. It loses its Yiddish inflection and her voice rings out as if she were speaking through a megaphone. But today I know that all these statements are intended for me.

"Never mind how old I am," she says. "Never mind when I was born. Or where, or to what mother. There's only one important fact about a life. And that one is always a beginning. A woman who lives for a cause, a woman with dedication and unbreakable devotion — that's a woman who deserves the name of woman."

Has she been rehearsing this little speech? I ask myself. Has she been going over it again and again in her mind, as she waited for me at the airport?

As we leave the table she looks out the window, bends her knees slightly, and tips back her head, trying to catch sight of the moon. "Not yet," she mutters and walks toward the room where Larissa has been building a fire.

Here, everything has a story. The charcoal sketch of Harriet Tubman, given to her by Langston Hughes. The book of Tina Modotti's photographs, a gift from a young radical woman. And now I realize there is something new in this room, which she has been wanting me to notice. It is visible in the light from the small lamp attached to an oil painting of my sister in her red Komsomol scarf. It says:

TO ROSE CHERNIN FOR 25 YEARS OF MILITANT LEADERSHIP TO THE COMMITTEE FOR THE DEFENSE OF THE BILL OF RIGHTS. IN APPRECIATION OF YOUR LIFELONG DEVOTION AND STRUGGLE ON BEHALF OF THE FOREIGN-BORN AND ALL VICTIMS OF POLITICAL AND RACIAL OPPRESSION. PRESENTED AT THE 25TH ANNUAL BANQUET, JANUARY 18, 1974.

She watches me as I study the plaque, unconsciously reciting the words aloud to Larissa. Then she waves at it with a disparaging shake of her hand. "So what else could they say? You think someone would write: 'To Rose Chernin: A Mean Person'?"

She is standing next to the fire, her foot on the rocker of Gertrude's chair. They are twisting newspaper into tight coils. Larissa pokes at the glowing coals with a wire hanger. But my mother has been waiting to speak with me. And now she says, "My mother knew how to read and to write. Isn't it so, Gertrude? Mama was a literate woman."

This fact makes no impression upon my daughter. She has no context for wondering at this achievement, so rare, so remarkable in a Jewish woman of the shtetl. On me, however, these words make a tremendous impression. The tone in which my mother speaks them moves me even to tears. "Mama was a literate woman," she repeats with a strangely wistful pride. Now she looks significantly at me and I know that we have come finally to the end of all this hinting.

"You are a writer," she says. "So, do you want to take down the story of my life?"

I am torn by contradiction. I love this woman. She was my first great aching love. All my life I have wanted to do whatever she asked of me, in spite of our quarreling.

She's old, I say to myself. What will it take from you? Give this to her. She's never asked anything from you as a writer before. Give this. You can always go back to your own work later.

But it is not so easy to turn from the path I have imagined for myself. This enterprise will take years. It will draw me back into the family, waking its ghosts. It will bring the two of us together to face all the secrets and silences we have kept. The very idea of it changes me. I'm afraid. I fear, as any daughter would, losing myself back into the mother.

I sit down on the edge of the gray chair that used to be my father's favorite reading place. It occurs to me that I should reason with her, tell her how much it means to me now to go my own way. "Mama," I say, intending to bring everything out into the open. And then she turns toward me expectantly, a raw look of hope and longing in her eyes.

I learned to understand my mother's life when I was a small girl, waiting for her to come home in the afternoons. Each night I would set the table carefully, filling three small glasses with tomato juice while my father tossed a salad. Then we would hear my mother's car pull up in front of the house and I could go into the living room and kneel on the gray couch in front of the window to watch her come across the lawn, weighed down with newspapers and pamphlets and large blue boxes of envelopes for the mailing I would help to get out that night.

She was a woman who woke early, no matter how late she went to bed the night before. Every morning she would exercise, bending and lifting and touching and stretching, while I sat on the bed watching her with my legs curled up. Then, a cold shower and she would come from it shivering, smelling of rosewater, slapping her arms. She ate toast with cottage cheese, standing up, reading the morning paper. But she would always have too little time to finish her coffee. I would watch her taking quick sips as she stood at the door. "Put a napkin into your lunch," she'd call out to me, "I forgot the napkin." And there was always a cup with a lipstick stain standing half full of coffee on the table near the door.

Later, the Party gave her a car and finally she learned how to drive it. But in the early years she went to work by bus. Sometimes when I was on vacation I went downtown with her.

In her office she took off her shoes and sat down in a wooden chair that swiveled. Always, the telephone was ringing. A young black man. Framed on a false murder charge. And so she was on her feet again, her fist clenched. By twelve o'clock she would have made friends with the young man's mother. And for years after that time some member of his family would drive across town on his birthday to pick up my mother and take her home to celebrate.

It was the invariable pattern of her life, as I learned to know it when I was a little girl, still hoping to become a woman like my mother. To this day I rise early, eat a frugal meal, take a cold shower and laugh as I slap my arms, bending and stretching, touching and reaching.

But I cannot describe my day with these bold, clear strokes that sketch in her life. This strange matter of becoming a poet, its struggle so inward and silent. How can I tell her about this life that has so little to show for itself in the outer world?

But I should never underestimate my mother. Since I was a child she has been able to read my thoughts. And now she turns from the bookshelf where she has been showing my daughter the old books she brought back during the thirties from the Soviet Union. She looks at me with that serious, disapproving gaze which taught me, even as a small child, always to lie about myself. And now she comes toward me, in all the extraordinary power of her presence, to touch me with her index finger on my shoulder.

"I went to Cuba last year," she says. "I took with me . . . what was it? Twenty-five people. All of them younger than myself. And you know what they did at night? Did I tell you? They went to sleep. Now could I sleep in a place like that? I ask you. So I took this one and that one, we went out into the streets, we walked, we went into restaurants. I don't care what the doctors tell me. I'm not going to rest. Do I have to live to be a hundred? What matters to me, so long as I'm living, I'm alive."

For me, these words have all the old seductive charm I experienced as a small girl, learning to know this woman. I loved her exclamation of surprise when someone came to our door, her arms flying out, her pleasure at whoever it was, dropping in on the way to a meeting. It was open house at our house on Wednesday nights. We never knew who might drop in. We'd pull up an extra chair, my father would go off to add lettuce to the salad, I'd pour another glass of tomato juice, and my mother would climb up on a stepladder to bring down a tin of anchovies. Every Wednesday morning she prepared a big pot of beef stroganoff or a spaghetti sauce with grated carrots and green pepper, which I would heat up, to simmer slowly, when I came home from school.

But how could I become my mother? She arrived in this country as a girl of twelve. An immigrant, struggling for survival, she supported her family when her father ran off and deserted them. To me she gave everything she must have wanted for herself, a girl of thirteen or fourteen, walking home from the factory, exhausted after a day of work.

What she is grows up out of her past in a becoming, natural way. She was born in a village where most women did not know how to read. She did not see a gaslight until she was twelve years old. And I? Am I perhaps what she herself might have become if she had been born in my generation in America?

This thought, although it remains unspoken, startles my mother. She looks over at me as if I have called her. And now she reaches out and pats my face, her hand falling roughly on my cheek.

She clears her throat. There comes into her voice a strangely confessional tone. "I'd come into your room at night," she says, "there you'd be. Looking out the window." She breathes deeply, shaking her head at some unpleasant impression life has left upon her. "I thought, this one maybe will grow up to be a *Luftmensch*. You know what it means? A dreamer. One who never has her feet on the ground."

She stops now, looking at me for understanding. She is vulnerable, uncertain whether she can continue. "We were poor people. Immigrants. For everything we had to struggle." I do not take my eyes from her face. And then the words rush from her, their intensity unexpected, shattering both of us. "The older I get the more I think about Mama. Always I struggled. Never to be like Mama. Never like that poor, broken woman . . ."

Larissa has been taking books out of the bookshelves, stacking them up on the floor, overturning the stacks. She seems surprised at the crash as her face turns toward her grandmother, who nods conciliation, as she never did to me, the child of her anxious years.

My grandmother could not adjust to the New World. I

79

have heard this all my life. She was sent to a mental hospital. She attempted suicide. My mother would talk about the beautiful letters she wrote. "A Sholom Aleichem," my mother would say. "The most heartbreaking stories," my aunt echoed. Then she added. "She must have wanted to become a writer."

She, too, was a dreamer and she lived through most of her days in that sorrow of mute protest which in her generation was known as melancholia. My mother, her daughter, was obsessed by the fate of her mother and this obsession has descended to me. But who could have imagined these old stories would awaken my child to an interest in the family? She is growing up, I say to myself, she is becoming conscious, my heart already stirred by the magnitude of this, she is entering the mythology of this family.

The twilight comes into the room. It spreads itself out on the stacks of magazines, the lacquered Chinese dish, the little carved man with a blue patch in his wooden trousers. Everyone begins to look as if they have been brushed with understanding. For here finally is the clear shape of the story my mother wants me to write down — this tale of four generations, immigrants who have come to take possession of a new world. It is a tale of transformation and development — the female reversal of that patriarchal story in which the power of the family's founder is lost and dissipated as the inheriting generations decline and fall to ruin. A story of power.

My mother has stopped talking. She raises her eyebrows, asking me to respond to her. Soon I know if I hold silence she will take a deep breath and straighten her shoulders. "Daughter," she will say, in a voice that is stern and admonishing, "always a woman must be stronger than the most terrible circumstance. You know what my mother used to say? Through us, the women of the world, only through us can everything survive."

An image comes to me. I see generations of women

bearing a flame. It is hidden, buried deep within, yet they are handing it down from one to another, burning. It is a gift of fire, transported from a world far off and far away, but never extinguished. And now, in this very moment, my mother imparts the care of it to me. I must keep it alive, I must manage not to be consumed by it, I must hand it on when the time comes to my daughter.

Larissa tugs at my sleeve. She is pointing to the window. I wonder why I feel such shame that I am crying, why I want to hide my face in my hands. I see my mother standing by the window, the dark folds of the drape gathered on either side of her. And there, above her head, where my daughter is now pointing, we see the slender cutting of a sickle moon, as my mother stands in silence, her arms folded upon her breast.

My mother sighs. But even in this expression of weariness or sorrow, I feel the power of the woman, as she straightens her shoulders, strides back into the room, sits down on the coffee table in front of me, and takes my hands.

"You never knew how to protect yourself," she says, "You never knew. I would stand there and watch you weep. You wept for everything. The whole world seemed to cause you pain. And I would say to myself, This one I will strengthen. This one I will make a fighter. And you, why can't you forgive me I wanted to teach you how to struggle with life? Why can't you forgive?"

My head moves down. I cannot restrain myself any longer. I know what I am going to do and I must take the risk. I feel my own lips, cold, unsure of themselves, pressed against my mother's hand. Very softly, whispering, I say to her, "Mama, tell me a story."

She lifts her head, her breast rises. "Good," she says. "From the mother to the daughter."

And so, eagerly now, I surrender. Deeply moved, I shall do what she has asked. I sit down on the floor, leaning against the knees of a white-haired old woman. And yes, with all the skill available to me as a writer, I will take down her tales and tell her story.

She was born in the first years of this century, in that shtetl culture which cannot any longer be found in this world. Her language is that haunting mixture of English, Yiddish, and Russian, in which an old world preserves itself. It is a story that will die with her generation. My own child will know nothing of it if it is not told now.

How could I have imagined that I, who am one of the few who could translate her memory of the world into the language of the printed page, had some more important work to do?

It grows dark as she is talking. "Today I will tell you about my life as a child," she says. "But the beginning, who can tell you? I don't know even the day I was born." No one moves to turn on the light. Far away, there is the sound of barking. And now, from a darkness no one of us wishes ever to visit, a wolf lifts its head and begins to howl. But none of this matters to me now. I am safe here in this little house. A cock crows at the edge of the village. The goat coughs in the cellar and on the windowsill there is a baked potato, cut in half and holding a candle someone has just lighted.

"When we were coming to America we made up the date for my birth. 'Rochele, Rochele,' my mother would say, pointing to me. 'First born. A daughter.' Then she would take hold of her ear. 'Do you remember, Papa? She was born when there was standing no more wheat in the field.'"

For a moment she catches her breath; her eyes dart uncertainly from me to the picture of my sister, above the fireplace, and back to me again.

But I — I am the one who has been chosen to set these stories down.

"And so they reconstructed. My grandfather picked out a date. September 14, 1903. You think this will do for a beginning?"

Uterus

LINNEA JOHNSON

She called me Uterus. I think she meant to name me "Eunice," but she didn't; she named me Uterus. But then, she spoke of my father as if he were a revolver; she'd say, "You know, Uterus, a man of your father's caliber, he . . ." and she would go on to describe him —long in the snout, a hair trigger. He was forty-five years old when I was born, but not my mother. She was sixty-three and still had regular menses as she would announce to the butcher. She noticeably oiled her body as if she were a weightlifter; "Got leather cupcakes for boobs," she'd say. And she was proud of me, prouder still of having had me when she did. Photos show and I remember her holding me up showing me off like a Campbell's commercial might a fine new can of soup, me all dolled up in lace and what looked like doilies. The Ivory baby. She'd said I looked like the Ivory flakes baby.

One Friday night when my mom and dad and I had settled onto the living room couch for an evening's television, she said she thought she should be the one in the filmy nightygown selling Frigidaires on that evening game show. "Your dad, well, Uterus, he could be up on a horse selling Marlboros he's so good looking." She lit one up, sucked the filtered end of it, then tongued off the lipstick she'd left on it. "He could sell 'em mounted on a burro. What a man. From on top a burrito! Right, Daddy?" She nudged at him from behind me. But Daddy got up, twisted the center of his boxer shorts over to his left so nothing would fall out the seamed slit and went out to the kitchen for a beer wishing we were watching the fights instead of that evening game show. Better, anyway, than the pop tune countdown show, I think he thought. I watched the nylon frieze markings on the backs of his one-muscle thighs as he walked away from us. My mother squashed out the Marlboro on the inner pink of the conch-shell-with-legs she used for an ashtray. She mostly didn't smoke.

This was a Friday night during the spring I was seven. My father would have been fifty-two by then, in that case. It was coming up on my mother's seventieth birthday. She thought she was pregnant again, wanted it, spent most of the balmy April nights ironing my old baby flannel things. My father said, "it's your imagination" to which my mother replied, "That's what you said about her" — meaning me — "is she my imagination?" For a long time I thought I was or might be just that but then she wasn't talking to me, so I didn't have to pretend to know the answer. My father wouldn't answer. My mother would stroke her belly; really raise her blouse or T-shirt to stroke her belly.

Early that April she'd set up the ironing board in the living room next to the couch to one side of the TV so she could be with us while she could still be ironing all my old baby clothes. She hummed and sang. I thought she was beautiful, her full face an indecision of skin and bone. She stood me up on an orange crate next to her, put the iron on low, low heat and taught me the intricate art of ironing — first the sleeves, then the back, then the collar, around any buttons, then each of the front sides. There were long sacques like Sweet Pea wore in the cartoons; I liked those best. Those and the tiny white flannel head caps with the narrow pastel satin ties which the point of the iron uncurled, flattened, and made shimmery and lank as a piece of weighted tinsel. She told me what I had been like in each thing we ironed, what a cute baby head I'd had and how exactly it fitted into her hand, heavy back weight of it in the cup of her palm. She would hold out her hand and look at it, form it to what she remembered to have been there, my cute babyhead. "And never once did you spit up. That's how happy you were." We were ironing the bibs. She'd embroidered the ducks and dragons on them herself.

"I never iron, do I? This is special. Feel this belly. Full of somebody who'll really like these clothes." For ironing the sheets she put her hand over mine and we sailed the stripes and bears of their length and breadth. "You were the damndest sweet baby. Long enough in coming, Uterus. They put you up to my breast that first time, you damn near sucked it off. What a kid." We ironed. Back and forth. Then we folded. My father would sit on the couch and watch the succession of commercials and programs. She jiggled her fingers through my ginger curls. "Tell her she's quite a kid, Pappa Ooo-mau-mau." He would.

Somebody asked me the other day if there were trees there in South Chicago when and where I grew up. I remember there had been light poles, general timber utility poles which had been treated with something, creosote, maybe, from the ground up about six feet. Around such things was always a brown mat of weeds and wads of variously decomposing dog-poo. Sparrows seemed to live on the wires in alternating shifts with other darker birds. Pigeons were further downtown and along the el tracks where stood the penny red-peanut machines. Peanuts for them, Chicklets front-tooth gum for us; the little square glass machines sat side by side. It was robins my mother looked for that spring and each earlier spring that I could remember. Head out the window, face a searchlight, my mother wouldn't rest until she'd seen a robin. There must have been something besides telephone wires for them to sit on; there must have been trees. I simply don't remember the sense of trees when I was a kid; nothing of the leafy blessing they are to me now though young and short as I was then, perhaps my mother was all the tree I needed (or noticed) then. If they were there, trees and birds, they had to have been hearty creatures. My mother. That sky was a mix of steel shards and alkaline dust, malt and petroleum vapors, ship exhaust and airborne waterway sewage. I remember sky and some snow as red; grey, mostly. I don't remember anyone in my neighborhood raking leaves. Laundry we hung up to dry in the basement, sheets stiff from the lack of breeze, grey as if they'd been dried outside. For me, if spring wasn't the sight of new-leafed trees, it was the sight of an apartment full of lace curtains stretched on wood and nail frames drying in the basement.

The apartment was nice. It had windows that opened, sash cords mostly intact. We lived up a flight so we weren't eyeball to eyeball with the street traffic which wasn't then what it would be now; then it was mostly kids on scooters or hefting bats, swearing a little, smoking in alleys as dusk swirled around their gym shoes. The Robert Hall sign a block up the street from our five rooms stayed on all night so we really saved on electricity, as my father liked to point out to my mother, re-confirming repeatedly his choice of a place to live, I guess. The lake was pretty close though the park preceding the lake overshadowed the joys of the lake for me when I was a kid; the swings were, after all, not out in the water but in the park's sparse grass. The harbor was closer than the lake or the park, unfortunately, though I liked to watch the tankers spill oil and take on wheat and occasionally blow up from the bulk or dust of it. The brewery grain elevators went up more frequently but they were farther down the Skyway. Kids who lived farther south, on the East Side, could watch, feel, and smell the Shell oil tanks blow up way over in East Chicago, Indiana. But I couldn't see that from just a second floor apartment in South Chicago. But the whole southern rim of the poorer lake neighborhoods went to the same park and from the WPA stone walls we could all sit and watch the steel mills red-up the sky summer nights when it was too hot to do anything else in or outside any apartment.

My mother acted like she really liked the place, putting up gardenia wallpaper one year, painting the kitchen a robin's egg blue another time. She dusted windowsills and seemed to look forward to washing and stretching and then rehanging the lace curtains every spring. It had a bedroom and a little sun porch off the dining room which had always been my room; it was wonderful spring and fall though in Chicago the other two seasons are rougher and a good deal longer.

The kitchen had a porcelain sink on legs with a window over it. She polished the chrome legs of the kitchen table and put an oilcloth over it, each tablecloth lasting until it cracked, chipped, and wore through to the bare weave. I liked the back porch stairway best. And, like I said, the windows opened.

So, this April we spent ironing baby clothes, my father skeptical, my mother nearly seventy and growing a belly which was hard and thumped like a watermelon. She sewed seersucker slacks for herself, an accordion fan of material up from the crotch to the waist to accommodate the growth, a string inside the waistband to be tied in a neat bow above her belly button. She sewed a couple extra pair because of the vacation my father had been planning and which, no matter when she was due, she said she would let nothing spoil. She kept the sewing machine on the sun porch so, as it was my bedroom, I was in on much of the sewing of her clothes. "This vacation's for your dad, he works hard, he does," she'd say, the pump of the sewing machine pushing the sweet smell of machine oil up into my room. Out of my sight, maybe, but I'd never seen him lift a finger in the seven years I'd been alive. "Feel this kid, Uterus. Here's the head." She always wanted me to touch the outside for the baby inside but I only would when she would take my hand, her hand on top of it and move my hand over the thing like the way the Navy moves a mine sweep over the Pacific. I couldn't feel or hear anyone kick or move or hum; she said she could hear the baby hum. Sing somethings. Little tunes: "Onward Christian Soldiers" was one tune she could hear the baby singing; she would cock her head, ear down towards her belly, eyes closed until she could pick up the tune, nod her head to the beat, and join in. "Yes, your father has always wanted to go westering. This is the year we're going to do it. They get restless, men do. So it's you and me and the baby and your dad." Sometimes she would press the side of my head to her; could I at least hear the water slosh she would ask of me. I couldn't and I felt disobedient for the first time in my life. My father sided with me and I didn't like that either. I loved my mother very much.

Her birthday was June 12th; that June 12th she would be seventy. My father and I took the bus over to Roseland to shop; mother knew all the stuff at the Robert Hall and at the South Chicago Sears store, he said; we had to go elsewhere. He didn't know what to get her and I felt strange going anywhere without her. I told him to get her a filmy nightygown and I wanted, please, some hot cashews if they had a nut counter anywhere in Roseland half as nice as the nut counter in the Sears store by our house. It was at this point my father decided to tell me just how old seventy was to him and that "... you can stop ironing them babyclothes. Nothing in there she's going to bring home from a hospital," he said, his hand around my wrist at the five and dime store soda counter.

"Want a chocolate phosphate?" Just then a lady who looked like she sold things sat down next to him and he kissed her. "Beatrice, meet Felicia Oleander." He called me the wrong name or maybe I just didn't recognize my name in his mouth being handed as if it were on a platter to this eggplant-faced woman who laid her arm across my daddy's belly like it was a guard pole from a Ferris wheel seat at Riverview, her hand wiggling its fingers as if they were zealous worms trying to attract a fish — my hand in this case. "How do you do," I said, my mother's daughter, always polite. "Who's she?" I said, growing up.

But he turned towards her and I ran away to see which of the parakeets were alive, which of the fish, my face hot, wet, and as distended as my mother's belly, me there in a strange store in a strange part of the world. I couldn't get home without him, though then and there I did rehearse my address and phone number should I be able to find one of the nice policemen my mother had always told me I could rely on if ever I found myself lost; if ever I was lost, it was then. Eventually I went back to the soda counter but I couldn't look at him ever again. And I didn't. I saw him for years, of course. He and Felicia raised me after my mother died, a month short of her seventieth birthday, no baby inside her, all those baby clothes ironed, folded, waiting. When she went away to the hospital in pain early that May I readied everything should she and the baby or she or just the baby come home; if it were only the baby I would raise it alone. Quiet as it was inside her, it would be no trouble. I already knew how to iron. I could probably sew from watching her. My mother and I were so close, maybe she'd taught me everything I already needed to know. We'd be fine. I would name it Robin. I managed to tuck most of those clothes into the closed end of my mother's casket. Felicia, who really was pregnant, wasn't going to get my mother's work. Not if I could help it. And I could.

That April day Felicia bought me hot cashews and chocolate candy none of which I ate; she helped my father pick out a housedress for my mother. "Save the receipt," Felicia said to my dad.

When I got home, my mother thought I was sick. She took me from my father's grip, felt my forehead, and bundled me off to a hot bath. She dug through my drawers and retrieved from the winter things last year's flannel jammies which, after she'd toweled me off, she dressed me in. By that time it was getting dark and my father had gone out to get some beer for evening television. That night my mother and I sat in the big old chair by the front room window and I told her I could hear the baby singing; what was she going to name the baby and was it going to be another girl like me, or just a boy. She sang "Uterus, there will never be another you," and said, "But it's a girl. Why we've got enough trouble in this world without bringing into it one more boy. I wouldn't have one, would you?"

She had beautiful full lips, my mother did, creased from years of lipstick, talk, and kissing, she liked to say. She was warm that night as we sat squeezed together in the chair, me flanneled over, her in her old thick plaid robe which always smelled to me like we had dogs. She told me the story of the baby alligators people bring home from Florida and then when they get too big for the bathtubs, people flush them down toilets; the ones who survive all grow up in sewers. She'd grown up an orphan, she said and had always felt like a half-grown baby alligator but crawling out of the sewer onto the streets. She laughed and showed me the skin on her neck to prove her alligatorness, the intricate wrinkles of the skin on the top of her hands at rest. "What d'ya think," she asked me as she snapped her hands together palm of one on top of the other imitating an alligator mouth. "Scary?"

"No," I said, but that night I was scared.

She laughed and said she'd crawled around the world a couple times, sometimes on her belly, sometimes on her back.

"Had a ball," she said, "Had a ball." She left the lights off that night, allowing the Robert Hall dark to filter in until what we were to each other was pure sound, our bodies pushed together in that chair, joined as if we were one again.

"Ah, but then I turned sixty and I'd done everything but have myself you." So, at sixty, she decided to marry someone seeing as she'd not done that before and given that she thought she would like to have me. She found my father and never found him out. He clerked shoes at the Wiebolt's. She'd accumulated a little what she called "nest egg" that provided just about exactly her half the rent and utilities so after she had me she didn't go back to sterilizing surgical instruments at South Chicago Hospital or selling tickets to the coal mine ride at the Museum of Science and Industry or back to any of the other ways she'd spent the first sixty years of her life. She liked to think she was the only one on Social Security pension who had their own born seven year old.

That April night she rocked me almost to sleep, my head falling from her shoulder to her big belly. I told her I could hear the baby singing "When The Moon Comes Over The Mountain" just like a teeny Kate Smith. I said, too, she had a filmy nightygown coming as her birthday present. She fluffed my hair, tipped my face up to her with two ruby red finger-nails and said, "You know, Uterus, I feel like a whole carton of cigarettes I'm so Lucky!"

Giving My
Mother A Bath

MARY JANE MOFFAT

Mid-morning of her third day home from the hospital with a new hip, I rig up this contraption in her bathtub — a wooden stool that rests on the pull-out kitchen breadboard for a stable base. In her walker she backs up to the tub and I guide her broad white rump onto the stool. She swings her good leg over the side and down into the easeful water. "Oh my," she sighs. "This feels so fine."

The right leg she can't yet bend sticks out over the rim like a useless oar. I scan the tiny bathroom for a prop — we're too far into this precarious enterprise to quit now. My overnight case I've stashed under the sink looks the right height. With my toe I slide it under her bad leg. If she asked me for some trinket in Tiffany's window, I think I'd smash plate glass with my bare hands to grab it for her. But all she wants is a bath.

Slowly I soap the cloth with Dove. I haven't seen her naked in a long time. "My how you've grown," I say.

She pats her belly-mound. "Let's face it. I am *fat*."

Ever since the arthritic hip began to hurt so much she gave up walking beyond the mailbox on her front porch, her restless energy has focused on eating. She treats every meal like a miracle. A dab of gravy trembling on her chin, she'll declare. "This must be the best food God ever put on this earth"; her eyes greedily check the serving dishes for seconds.

I hold up the washcloth. "Where shall we begin?"

She shuts her eyes and thrusts out her homely mug for my lathered blessing. I remember how I squirmed at the rough kiss of her spit on a hankie when she rubbed soot from my cheeks. Now, her brow untroubled, she submits to my soaping; her very pores seem open to whatever may come.

Through the cloth I memorize her face. At seventy-eight, her wrinkles aren't as deeply incised as mine, although compared to the sorrows and hardships she's endured, most of my life has seemed trivially easy. For one thing, I've always had her; she was six when her own mother died.

With my ring finger I pat the pouches under her eyes and smooth the lines that river from the roots of her nose into tiny creeks at the corners of her mouth. I wipe away traces of yesterday's lipstick and feel the lump of calcification that protects a speck of glass buried in her lower lip — on a rainy night ten years ago, she swerved to miss a motorcyclist and went through the windshield of her Buick. The lump gives her mouth, in repose, a stubborn look at odds with her bonny disposition. I have an unforgivable thought: she's going to look angry in her casket.

Under the loose skin of her high cheekbones, I feel the shape of the skull that will survive, as probably somewhere still lie buried the wide-malared skulls of our ancestors who drove herds across central Asia into the Finnish north.

I press the browbones above her eyes, smoothing upward the skimpy hairs she fills in with pencil.

"That feels real good," she says. She thinks I'm giving her a massage. With my other hand, I rub the knot of muscles at the base of her neck. I know exactly how to do it so the nerves cry out with pleasure. Early on, when she rubbed my neck with her big-knuckled fingers in the exact spots where I hurt, I realized that she and I tighten up in all the same places. Even when she sleeps, she doesn't look relaxed but in a hurry.

"You should try and sit up straight." I pull back her shoulders and feel the resistance of the hump her spine is curving toward. Briefly she straightens, sighs "Ah, Gahd," and slumps again, yielding to gravity's seductive tug. I pull back my own shoulders.

"Water too cold?"

"A little," she admits.

"Why didn't you say so?"

She shrugs.

"I'm not going to wash your hair."

"So don't. Big deal," she says.

Before the surgery, Phoebe the beautician gave her an unfortunate "wash & wear" cut — two inches at its longest — and permanented her fine hair into feeble curls that look like the dust kittens under a bed. Now her exposed ears seem enormous.

"Actually, it's kind of cute," I say.

"Thank you very much," she says drily. "Thanks a thousand." Her vanities are unpredictable. "Do you think we could get on with this?"

I soap her neck wattles and bail palmsful of water into the hollows of her mended collarbone. When she was eighteen, she broke it on a forbidden ride in Dexter Johnson's Model T. The steering wheel came off in Dexter's hands. She told me that he gaily kept turning the wheel in thin air as they careened down those washboard country roads singing "Nearer My God to Thee." Until the car smashed into a tree.

Dexter came out fine. She fractured her skull. For a year

after, her face was paralyzed. "God punished me," she says now, as she does every time this story gets told, "for disobeying my father."

"That's horse manure," I tell her.

The paralysis left her with a left eyelid that droops when she's tired and a crooked smile. I have that same smile. For years I believed that acquired traits can be inherited.

Even though he died of t.b. long before I was born, I've always been in love with the Dexter Johnson of this story. Who knows? If the steering column hadn't broken, he might have been my Daddy.

"That Dexter sure had *sisu*," I tell my mother. *Guts* in Finnish. Only more: guts and style.

"Just think. If Dexter Johnson had been my father, I'd be ten years older."

"Sweetie-pie, there's no way Dexter Johnson could have been your father. For one thing, my father would never have let me marry a Swede."

She gives me a mock-prissy toss of her head. "And we didn't *do* it back then, you know. Before marriage."

I doubt that without her bifocals she catches my smile. One thing we never talk about is that I was born less than seven months after my parents' wedding day.

She explained it once: "You were premature."

Seven pounds, six ounces, it says on my birth certificate. Lucky for her I didn't go full term.

I rinse the back of her neck. The new haircut reveals the port wine stain at the nape. I almost forgot that I have the same birthmark — the reason I wear my hair long enough to cover all but a drop of the wine. How can she think it matters that my birth came awkwardly early, when I am so indisputably hers?

Let her have her little secret. I've committed some folly here and there I hope my sons don't know about, or if they do know, have the grace and wits not to let on.

Her bra straps have forced tracks into her fleshy shoulders. I travel down and soap her huge breasts, pulling up their pliant weight to get at the skin over her ribs. Her skin is beautiful; not papery-sad but plumped out with inner shine.

"Boy. I sure am glad I didn't get your boobs," I tease.

She hoots. "Now you're glad. Don't you remember in high school stuffing Kleenex in your bra?"

"I remember when you bought me my first one. Daddy said, 'Will you please tell me why she needs a bra for those little walnuts?'"

She smiles indulgently. "Your father. Wasn't he funny?"

"Hilarious."

"I miss him." With cupped palms, she bounces her breasts a little, as if to give them some exercise before they have to be strapped in again. "Don't you miss him?"

Oh my. A hard question. To me, missing someone means to wish he were here right now, maybe in the next room, the way I miss my dead husband. The last several years of his life, my father was as difficult and manic-crazy as you can get without being locked up. If he were still alive, I doubt that she'd have survived these last five years.

She doesn't know I write stories about my girlhood so I can't tell her that often he comes into them, completely uninvited. I'm always glad to be with him again for awhile. I know exactly what he would say and I faithfully write it down, knowing I can send him away when I need to.

"Sure I miss him," I tell my mother. "But as he would say after Aunt Ida went home after a visit, 'it's a good miss.'"

"I bet you miss Larry," she says. "You poor kid. Having to drop everything to fly up here and work your fingers to the bone."

Larry is the man I live with — rather, who lives with me. When I first introduced him to her as "an old friend from Menlo Park," she was cool. That was the winter before my father's death when she'd had a mild stroke and I snatched her away to San Francisco to recuperate in peace at my place.

When Larry showed up every night at dinnertime, she'd say, "You sure seem to like the food around here, Roy." And when in the morning she found him reading the paper at the breakfast table: "Back so soon from Menlo Park, Earl?"

Then one day for no particular reason — except that perhaps she saw that he made me happy — she decided to love him. As is her style in that department, she didn't go halfway.

"It's funny," she muses now. "I think I loved Jack — God-rest-his-darling-soul — more than any mother-in-law ever loved a son-in-law. And now I do believe I love Larry just as much."

"You love everybody," I complain, a spoiled child still wanting to be her mother's only miracle. I've reached the nether of her belly and, suddenly dizzy from the steam or from bending, I hand over the washcloth.

"You do your *takapuoli* and your privates." I shunt around her walker and sit on the lid of the hospital-supply commode that elevates the toilet. While she obediently washes the mysterious and unspeakable regions from which I sprang, I stare at the stippled pink of the ceiling. It needs a coat of paint.

She waves the cloth to show she's finished her assignment. On my knees, I address the less complicated expanse of her back.

Two years ago the cancerous lobe of one lung was removed. Now the scar under her left shoulder blade is an almost imperceptible line, as if someone simply had run his fingernail across her flesh. I still regret that I couldn't come take care of her then. Her younger sister, the humorless and dutiful Ida, bussed down from Spokane. She'll come again in a few days when I have to leave.

"So what are you going to do to devil Aunt Ida this time?" The last convalescence, her sister lectured her so relentlessly about cigarettes causing the cancer that my mother, although she'd lost all nicotine-craving during her long hospital stay, forced herself to chain-smoke in Ida's presence.

"It almost killed me, but I did it," she told me on the phone when she reported that Ida had fled home in tears on the Greyhound."

"*Gahd,* that Ida," she says now. She scrooches up her face. "Can't you stay and spare me?"

"You know you love Aunt Ida."

She puts on her stubborn look. "Of course I love her. I just can't stand her."

The neat new scar on her lower back, where just three weeks ago another surgeon cut in and broke her hip to install the artificial one, looks almost healed. For comparison, I pull down the waistband of my jeans and show her my jagged forty-year-old appendix scar.

"See? Yours already looks better."

She clucks over my scar. "You poor kid. Back then they kept you a whole month in the hospital. You cried so hard when I left after visiting hours that I'd come home and cry all night."

I massage the nest of nerves on her tailbone. "I wasn't crying for you. I was weeping for my sins."

Between grunts of pleasure at what I'm doing to her coccyx, she says, "That's ridiculous. You've never sinned in your life. You were born perfect and you stayed that way."

"Oh I sinned all right. I lied about having a stomachache because I wanted to get out of my arithmetic class." To this day I associate long division with the smell of gas and postoperative retching.

"What are you talking about? You were a very sick girl."

I slosh water on her back and on my knees move around the overnight case to work on the foot that's in the water.

"My big mistake was saying the pain was on my right side. How was I to know that's where your appendix is? — I was only in fifth grade. Before I knew it, there I was in St. Vincent's with a scalpel poised over my perfect innards."

She grabs my wrist so fiercely I drop the cloth; with her other hand she takes my chin so I have to look her in the eye.

"Do you mean to tell me there was nothing wrong with you? Dr. Essex said your appendix was going to burst and you might die."

I try and reach back for how all this came about — it's been a long time.

"You had *Forever Amber* from the rental library hidden in your top drawer." She rarely took time to read books but everyone was talking about this one; and it had been denounced by the Methodist Board of Temperance and Morals which made it irresistible.

"I could tell from the bookmark that you were almost finished. And so I told the teacher I had this godawful stomachache so I could read how it turned out while you were at work. It cost ten cents a day — you were sure to return it the next morning."

She drops my wrist. "Well I'll be damned. I always thought that doctor with his Thomas Dewey moustache was a horse's *takapuoli.*" She breathes hard. "Why didn't you say you were faking? I would have believed you and put a stop to it."

I fish the cloth out of the scummy water and work on her hammertoes. The water has softened her corns and callouses; if I had a pumice stone handy, I probably could scour them away.

There's really no answer to her question. I'm in no mood now to blame my ten-year-old self for moral cowardice. Or on the other hand to give her much credit for accepting the radical consequences of her lie. Losing my appendix without cause just happened. Like so many human events that later take on emotional cargo, things had gone too far before I realized it *was* an event; and that I was trapped in it.

My mother rubs her brow with the heel of her hand. "I feel terrible — that you went through all that for nothing. I feel so guilty."

"If anyone, that rat-snout doctor should feel guilty." I pinch her big toe. "You've never done a single thing in your life you should feel guilty about."

Her left eye twitches. "You don't know half of it. It makes me sick that I worked when you were little. That you spent all that time alone in the apartment, growing up without brothers and sisters. And then about your father. . . ."

"I'm the one who should feel guilty about him. And you would have been bored silly staying home. It just so happens, I had a wonderful childhood." As soon as I say it, I realize that it's true. How tedious it would have been to grow up in a bland steady family like the one depicted in my first grade primer.

She gives a sad little laugh. "You can't understand because you're only half-Finnish. By nature, a Finlander is born feeling guilty. You tell us to jump, we ask, 'how high?'"

"Mother, I hate to disappoint you, but the Finns did not invent guilt."

"Yah? So who did?"

"I don't know. The Jews, I suppose. Moses and that crowd."

She sighs. "I guess I must be Jewish then."

"It's what I've always suspected. Let's face it — how many Methodists do you know with a decent sense of humor?"

"Aren't you *funny,*" she chides. "Just like your father."

"You have beautiful feet," I tell her.

"Are you kidding? I hate my ugly feet."

"Don't you dare hate those feet. Do you realize all they've done for you?"

I think of when she was a girl lonely for her mother and her feet carried her through the mud morning and night to milk the cows; the hand-me-down shoes they squeezed into; how they ran away to Seattle to escape her father's sin-obsessed Calvinism; the steps they've climbed; the errands for others they've run; when her hip heals, the heavy weight they still will bear.

"Praise these feet," I declaim, giving her a good show with the broad gestures I learned years ago in drama school. I plant a kiss on her unwashed foot that sticks out over the tub. "May these feet clump on forever!"

"Cut that out," she says, embarrassed. "Sometimes I swear you act as crazy as your father. Trying to make me feel guilty for insulting my dumb feet. Honestly."

I see how tired she is. Her breathing sounds like a mushy piston and her left eye droops at half-mast. She's clean enough, I decide, and I ease her good leg over the side of the tub and swaddle her in fluffy towels.

But when I try and hoist her from the stool, she's dead weight. Three times I try. Her arms clasped around my neck, she grunts and strains to help.

"Oh God," she cries out in anger. "How did I get so old?"

"Give me a minute," I say. "I'll think of something."

I sit on the commode. Patiently, her lower lip looking stubborn, she stares at the bathroom wall. The leaky faucet drips fresh water into the tub. No doubt the breadboard's warping away down there and will never fit back into its slot — what a dumb idea that was.

But my mind isn't puzzling the present problem. I've gone far back to when I used to sit on the toilet lid to be near her while she bathed before going to work.

She was thin then. Her full breasts rode high above the water line. Her lovely lopsided grin revealed her own teeth. When she kissed me goodbye, she smelled of Blue Grass, not the faint, dank vapors of age. She was never sick. And she was never, ever going to die.

Now she clears her throat. "I hate to tell you this" — she rolls her eyes with clownish urgency — "but I have to go to the *hysikka*."

"Mama, I don't know what to do." I can't even get her out of the tub, much less over to the toilet.

"You go out. Leave me alone. I can manage if I don't have to worry about you worrying."

"You might fall." She absolutely must not fall. The new hip could pop out of its socket like a boomerang.

"Am-scray," she says. "Right now."

I pick up the overnight case and push her walker closer to the tub and close the door behind me. From the hall I listen to her hum the first eight bars of "The Last Time I Saw Paris," over and over, the way she does when she's intent on a task. There's a couple of minor clunks, like plastic bottles falling on tile; when I hear the steady stream of her passing water, the sighs of her relief, I turn away from my cautionary eavesdropping and go into her room and turn down the bed.

After I hear the toilet flush, I give her a few minutes before I open the door. She wears the fresh blue nightie I had ready and, standing in her walker, she's busy teasing up her dust-kittens. Now that my eyes have adjusted, I decide the haircut really is pretty cute.

"How did you manage all that?" I help her maneuver the walker around the tight corner into her bedroom.

She looks terribly pleased with herself. "Oh I'm a tough old turkey. If you'd given me more time, I'd have scoured out my ring instead of leaving it for you."

She backs into her bed and I swing her legs up and arrange the sponge block under her thighs. This part I'm getting pretty good at. Her cheek burrows into the pillow and when I pull up the coverlet she sighs with happiness and closes her eyes.

I ask her what she wants for lunch.

Slyly, she opens one eye. "What do Jewish people like to eat?"

"How about gravlax on Swedish rye?"

She makes smacking noises with her lips.

"Hey. I could schlep down to Safeway and pick up a bottle

of Manischevitz."

"Whatever," sleepily she says.

"See you later."

My hand is on the doorknob when she says, "Wait a minute. I have to ask you. Something's been bothering me."

I think, here it comes: some small truth I later can take out and hold up to the light. "Now I'll tell you about my mother," I'll say to my grandchildren once they're born and old enough to be interested.

"Tell me," I say.

Her eyes stay closed. "Did you ever find out how *Forever Amber* ends?"

I give this matter some thought. "I guess not. When I left her, things looked dark. The king was sore at her and she was coming down with the pox — poor Amber." I don't say that I've reached an age where I don't need to know how some stories turn out.

"Don't worry," she says. "I remember it perfectly. It's hilarious the way she escapes to America. You'll laugh, I promise. Fix lunch now. When I wake up, I'll tell you all about it." And with at least one debt settled for now, she hurries off into the aloneness of her sleep.

How I Became a Poet

AUDRE LORDE

"Wherever the bird with no feet flew she found trees with no limbs."

When the strongest words for what I have to offer come out of me sounding like words I remember from my mother's mouth, then I either have to reassess the meaning of everything I have to say now, or re-examine the worth of her old words.

My mother had a special and secret relationship with words, taken for granted as language because it was always there. I did not speak until I was four. When I was three, the dazzling world of strange lights and fascinating shapes which I inhabited resolved itself in mundane definitions, and I learned another nature of things as seen through eyeglasses. This perception of things was less colorful and confusing but much more comfortable than the one native to my nearsighted and unevenly focused eyes.

I remember trundling along Lenox Avenue with my mother, on our way to school to pick up Phyllis and Helen for lunch. It was late spring because my legs felt light and real, unencumbered by bulky snowpants. I dawdled along the fence around the public playground, inside of which grew one stunted plane tree. Enthralled, I stared up at the sudden revelation of each single and particular leaf of green, precisely shaped and laced about with unmixed light. Before my glasses, I had known trees as tall brown pillars ending in fat puffy swirls of paling greens, much like the pictures of them I perused in my sisters' storybooks from which I learned so much of my visual world.

But out of my mother's mouth a world of comment came cascading when she felt at ease or in her element, full of picaresque constructions and surreal scenes.

We were never dressed too lightly, but rather "in next kin to nothing." *Neck skin to nothing?* Impassable and impossible distances were measured by the distance "from Hog to Kick 'em Jenny." *Hog? Kick 'em Jenny?* Who knew until I was sane and grown a poet with a mouthful of stars, that these were two little reefs in the Grenadines, between Grenada and Carriacou.

The euphemisms of body were equally puzzling, if no less colorful. A mild reprimand was accompanied not by a slap on the behind, but a "smack on the backass," or on the "bamsy." You sat on your "bam-bam," but anything between your hipbones and upper thighs was consigned to the "lower-region," a word I always imagined to have French origins, as in "Don't forget to wash your *l'oregión* before you go to bed." For more clinical and precise descriptions, there was always "between your legs" — whispered.

The sensual content of life was masked and cryptic, but

attended in well-coded phrases. Somehow all the cousins knew that Uncle Cyril couldn't lift heavy things because of his "bam-bam-coo," and the lowered voice in which this hernia was spoken of warned us that it had something to do with "down there." And on the infrequent but magical occasions when mother performed her delicious laying on of hands for a crick in the neck or a pulled muscle, she didn't massage your backbone, she "raised your zandalee."

I never caught cold, but "got co-hum, co-hum," and then everything turned "cro-bo-so," topsy-turvy, or at least, a bit askew.

I am a reflection of my mother's secret poetry as well as of her hidden angers.

Sitting between my mother's spread legs, her strong knees gripping my shoulders tightly like some well-attended drum, my head in her lap, while she brushed and combed and oiled and braided. I feel my mother's strong, rough hands all up in my unruly hair, while I'm squirming around on a low stool or on a folded towel on the floor, my rebellious shoulders hunched and jerking against the inexorable sharp-toothed comb. After each springy portion is combed and braided, she pats it tenderly and proceeds to the next.

I hear the interjection of *sotto voce* admonitions that punctuated whatever discussion she and my father were having.

"Hold your back up, now! Deenie, keep still! Put your head so!" Scratch, scratch. "When last you wash your hair? Look the dandruff!" Scratch, scratch, the comb's truth setting my own teeth on edge. Yet, these were some of the moments I missed most sorely when our real wars began.

I remember the warm mother smell caught between her legs, and the intimacy of our physical touching nestled inside of the anxiety/pain like a nutmeg nestled inside its covering of mace.

The radio, the scratching comb, the smell of petroleum jelly, the grip of her knees and my stinging scalp all fall into — *the rhythms of a litany, the rituals of Black women combing their daughters' hair.*

Saturday morning. The one morning of the week my mother does not leap from bed to prepare me and my sisters for school or church. I wake in the cot in their bedroom, knowing only it is one of those lucky days when she is still in bed, and alone. My father is in the kitchen. The sounds of pots and the slightly off-smell of frying bacon mixes with the smell of percolating Bokar coffee.

The click of her wedding ring against the wooden headboard. She is awake. I get up and go over and crawl into my mother's bed. Her smile. Her glycerine-flannel smell. The warmth. She reclines upon her back and side, one arm extended, the other flung across her forehead. A hot-water bottle wrapped in body-temperature flannel, which she used to quiet her gall-bladder pains during the night. Her large soft breasts beneath the buttoned flannel of her nightgown. Below, the rounded swell of her stomach, silent and inviting touch.

I crawl against her, playing with the enflanneled, warm, rubber bag, pummeling it, tossing it, sliding it down the roundness of her stomach to the warm sheet between the bend of her elbow and the curve of her waist below her breasts, flopping sideward inside the printed cloth. Under the covers, the morning smells soft and sunny and full of promise.

I frolic with the liquid-filled water bottle, patting and rubbing its firm giving softness. I shake it slowly, rocking it back and forth, lost in sudden tenderness, at the same time gently rubbing against my mother's quiet body. Warm milky smells of morning surround us.

Feeling the smooth deep firmness of her breasts against my shoulders, my pajama'd back, sometimes, more daringly, against my ears and the sides of my cheeks. Tossing, tumbling, the soft gurgle of the water within its rubber casing. Sometimes the thin sound of her ring against the bedstead as she moves her hand up over my head. Her arm comes down across me, holding me to her for a moment, then quiets my frisking.

"All right, now."

I nuzzle against her sweetness, pretending not to hear.

"All right, now, I said; stop it. It's time to get up from this bed. Look lively, and mind you spill that water."

Before I can say anything she is gone in a great deliberate heave. The purposeful whip of her chenille robe over her warm flannel gown and the bed already growing cold beside me.

"Wherever the bird with no feet flew she found trees with no limbs."

Excerpted from *Zami: A New Spelling of My Name*

Nicholas

HARRIET MALINOWITZ

"S urprise," I say.

It is.

For Nicholas is the last thing my mother expected, and I know that even in this first second she's seeing him wrong. I know what she thinks; I know how babies look through her eyes. She has no inkling of what he really is. I know I have the winning card in hand, to use whenever I want. I know. And she doesn't.

I tip the wheel of the stroller up the step into the living room, and lift him out, into my arms. I see her watching, hungrily, and I clutch him tightly to me. She is puzzled, distant, eager to reach for him, but my arms around him barricade her out. I possess him. She doesn't.

It is September, 1977, the month of my twenty-third birthday. In the East Village it is a cool, cloudy Wednesday afternoon. In my mother's house in Queens it is verging on

109

Yom Kippur, the Jewish day of atonement.

I have just taken a subway ride from Second Avenue, with Nicholas. On the train I sat in an aisle seat, with the stroller parked, brake on, beside me. I held onto it with one hand, while Nicholas dozed, drugged by the rhythm of the train. At Thirty-Fourth Street I looked up and saw Howard Weintraub hanging from a strap halfway down the car. He saw me at the same moment. We haven't seen each other since our graduation from high school five years ago, and after the first start of recognition had crossed his face there was a second shock, as he gaped at me and then Nicholas and back at me again. He pointed with his finger, his eyebrows lifting in amazement. I shook my head, laughing, and his shoulders heaved in mock relief before he pushed his way toward me. The second after I'd shaken my head no I wished I'd nodded instead, just for fun. Howard was dressed in a brown suit and tie, and he carried a briefcase. The first thing he said, after five years, was: "Going home for the holiday?" He told me he was an accountant and was getting married in June. I told him I was doing street theater satirizing capitalist patriarchy, and I explain about Nicholas. I saw a look of groping incertitude come to Howard's face that I'd never seen there once in four years of high school. I enjoyed the contrast between us. Very much.

This is the year I have decided to eclipse Yom Kippur. For years it has dragged me back, like childhood, an encumbrance that can't be shrugged off, or shed like a dead skin, so I could keep on metamorphizing. It doesn't matter if I travel to the ends of the earth, write great manifestoes, sleep with women, confront head-on the hells that lurk behind the stolid doorways of life; September still always comes and strips me of my guts, sucking me deep into its belly like a high-speed vacuum cleaner.

Obviously, I haven't been able to avoid it this year, for I

am here. But if Yom Kippur can intrude on me, so can I intrude on Yom Kippur. I have come, but Nicholas has come with me; and now I stand in the living room of my mother's house, which I still have to take care not to refer to accidentally as "my" house, with my arms protecting Nicholas, and Nicholas's small body protecting me.

"What's this?" exclaims my mother at last.

"A baby," I answer her.

She squints at me, drawing her head back a little.

"*Whose* baby?" she persists.

"A friend's," I say, sitting down in the rocker still wrapped in my woolen poncho, and beginning to rock to and fro with Nicholas in my lap, his deep brown eyes gazing into mine and mine into his. "A friend who's in the hospital. I *told* you I was bringing a surprise home for the holiday. Aren't you surprised?"

"I certainly am!" she agrees. Her irony is mixed with excitement. "Here, let me take him. . . ."

"It's OK, I've got him," I say, raising my elbow just in time to block her.

"What's his name?" she asks hurt, and hovering closely by at a loss, probably because no one has ever before challenged her in the realm of babies.

"Nicholas," I say. Just then Nicholas smiles at me, perhaps from hearing his own name, and I smile back.

"If your friend is in the hospital, where is Nicholas's father? Or shouldn't I ask?"

"You can ask," I say generously. "Nicholas's father is in Angola."

She is silent a moment.

"What is he doing in Angola, with a helpless infant and a wife in the hospital? Or — not a wife, maybe," she amends, almost apologetically, as if she knows me too well and is venturing this liberal hypothesis so I won't get my back up.

"He's a revolutionary," I reply.

Her eyes narrow. "Oh, and while he's busy starting the revolution it's OK for him to forget about his responsibilities to his child, and to his — I don't know her name, your friend —"

"He has no responsibilities to them. He has nothing to do with Nicholas's life. Ellen is essentially a single parent, if you must know." Of course she must know. Haven't I brought Nicholas here to prove it?

She grimaces and makes a sound to indicate her conviction that someone's personal craziness has been carried too far; that it is all very well to be idealistic and invent new ideas about families and relationships and children, but not to the point where you're actually tampering with *reality*—the kind of reality that is sitting in my lap in the rocking chair. I know that she is thinking this. I know she thinks Nicholas is the fruit of two overgrown children who have played with concepts that have nothing to do with what life is *really* about.

"And your friend—Ellen—has no family she can leave him with? Some familiar people who will care for him?"

"Her family is in St. Louis, and I'm more familiar to him than they are anyway. I'm perfectly capable of caring for him, or else I wouldn't have taken him."

"Couldn't her mother have flown in? I'm sure, if she knew her daughter was going into the hospital and the baby getting passed around from hand to hand. . . ."

"He's not getting passed around! He's with *me*! Besides, Ellen hasn't told her about the surgery. It's not a really big deal, and she hardly ever speaks to her, anyway."

"She hardly speaks to her mother?"

"That's right."

She pauses; then: "I'm *sure* her parents would want to know, especially if it concerned the welfare of their grandchild." Again, a beyond-all-shadow-of-a-doubt conviction.

"Anyway, they don't, and it's her decision."

She shakes her head. "It's pathetic," she says. I don't

know if she meant *it,* the situation, or *him,* in the dehumanizing way people sometimes speak of babies, but suddenly my anger turns to shame, my defiance to helplessness, and I quickly pass him to her. I cannot rid myself of him quickly enough. Suddenly, relegated to pathos, he feels like a contaminating substance in my arms and I need to make myself clean. "Here," I say, roughly, trying to press down the nausea that is welling inside me. I want to say, "There was no need to call him pathetic, but if you bring that up then you have to take responsibility for it."

But once he is in her arms, I see with mingled anger and relief, she is making him into an acceptable baby. She talks to him in her language, and he likes it. He smiles and gurgles appreciatively. I feel a little jealous that they are communicating so well. And a little outraged, that a baby of his origins could capitulate so easily! But I watch, waiting for her to do or say something that will retract what she has said before: "I was wrong — he's not pathetic, after all!" She is taking such obvious pleasure in holding him that I feel this is established.

She returns him to me so that she can heat up his milk. I hold him more comfortably now; things are a little clearer now. I want to remove my poncho and gently, carefully, I place him on the sofa. I slip the woolen folds over my head and quickly, quickly move to the closet, not removing my eyes for a second yet feeling wrong —

"*Shelley*!" I know this tone. I know what it means and it confirms what I have been feeling wrong about for these last few seconds. I am filled with anger — hopeless, impotent rage that I have brought Nicholas here to help me express, only apparently that was a mistake, too, for she has taken him from the sofa. She is armed; I'm not.

"You don't leave a baby alone on a sofa!" she says, and I say, "*You* don't!" and she says, exasperatedly, "Oh, *Shelley*!" I want to cry, "You see! You see! I'm sure you never left me on a sofa, and that's why I'm afraid of everything!" but then

I realize you can't say things like that, and I wonder how I can make her see it without saying it. I can't. Instead, she is making me see; I am feeling sick and miserable about the careless thing I have just done so deliberately.

The relatives come and they are delighted with Nicholas. "Who is he?" they want to know, and I feel censorious waves emanating from my mother—who is in the kitchen, arranging chopped eggs and onions inside a circle of Tam Tams on a plate — telling me not to defile the healthy Jewish holiday atmosphere with the truth about Nicholas. I explain, scrupulously honest, that Ellen met Nicholas's father, a Brazilian, in Portugal during the revolution in 1975; and that she became pregnant on purpose and wrote to him from New York, asking him how he would feel knowing he had a child whose life he would have no part in. He wrote back that he felt fine about it. She had the baby in her Soho loft with a midwife and me there to help.

I make it clear that Ellen has freely chosen all this.

As my relatives digest this information, I decide to stop and leave it at that. They are looking at me in the way they sometimes do when I am not yielding to their mentalities. There is a puzzled look in their eyes that distances them from me, that makes me feel a great gulf between us. I have purposely created this gulf, yet I am suddenly seized by an unreasonable desire to swim it. I look from face to face, cringing at the baffled disapproval I see. When I glance at my aunt Sarah I am startled to see awe in her expression. This is the trump I have been looking for, yet it disturbs me. Perhaps I don't want to be taken seriously after all? Perhaps I want to be convinced, like the rest of them, that the world of Nicholas is just an imaginary world? But no, then I'm wrong again, and Nicholas is here to help me put an end to being wrong like this all the time.

Dinner is over; everyone has begun fasting. They will fast until three stars appear in the sky tomorrow night. I let it slip, accidentally on purpose, that I will not fast. I'll humor them, as I have always been urged to do, and pretend to fast, yet it is understood that when no one is looking I will eat. Nicholas begins to cry. Everyone wants to hold him. Everyone thinks she has the magic touch, the special comfort to quiet him. After he has screamed for half an hour they lose patience, and I find that I have him all to myself. I take him in the den and pace up and down the room, jostling and soothing him. He does not stop. I check his diaper; he is dry, but there is a massive redness between his legs where inexperienced hands have fastened the diaper so it chafes. I remove the diaper and rub in ointment. Everyone piles into the den, making silly sounds, and he lies there happy in his nakedness, giggling up at the looming faces. He is not circumcised. "He doesn't realize that this is probably the only Yom Kippur he'll ever have," someone says. As if hereafter he will be deprived.

In spite of this, I feel happy now. I feel like the happy vortex, the point where east meets west, where Nicholas meets my family. This disappears when my mother gathers him once again into her arms and says with a renewed note of chagrin, "The poor thing!"

"*Stop* that!" I cry passionately. "He's fine! There's nothing wrong with him!" But my stomach has begun to lurch again. I wish I had never done this. I don't want to hear my mother's voice but I am helpless to erase it; like a black box intact after an explosion it remains with me, intransigent against time, against soul.

Valentine's Day

VALERIE MINER

St. Valentine, Priest and Martyr
Green, Purple or Red Vestments

Janet woke suddenly. She could tell, even with the blinds closed, that it was early on a cold day. Well, February was unpredictable in San Francisco. And Valentine's Day was unpredictable anywhere. She felt a stab of self-pity about her solitary state and snuggled under the covers. No, she was wide awake. She would make the most of this morning because she was behind on her taxes and on her tapestry orders. Christ! The Federal Express truck was supposed to collect the last piece for the Montreal gallery this morning and she hadn't even completed the address form.

She grabbed her robe, filled the kettle and sat at her desk to deal with questions of weight and destination. The form was pleasantly bilingual. She preferred to imagine herself as an *"expediteur"* rather than a "shipper." There was some small pleasure in addressing the gallery owner as a "consignee," which seemed to make them more equal.

The kettle blew. The phone rang.

"Hello, Mom?"

"Oh, Winnie, can you hang on while I get the stove?"

Checking the kitchen clock, she was startled to find her daughter calling at eight a.m. Since going to college Winnie had become a late sleeper.

"Mom, I wondered if I could come and use your computer today."

"I was planning to do my books on the computer, but I could sort through the files while you use it. I mean if you don't need my help. I'm way behind on taxes. You have an assignment?"

"No. My resumé. Companies are doing on-campus interviews next week. Are you sure it's OK?"

"Yeah, sure." She closed her eyes. It wouldn't hold her up that much. It might even be nice to have some company. She missed her only child.

Janet finished the form and put the tapestry in a box which she zealously swathed with translucent tape to ensure safe arrival. After this, there was nothing she could do. She felt as if she were sending it off to war.

She sat at the table with a second cup of coffee, marvelling at how small this looked for six months' work. Just another hanging to be put on just another wall.

The phone rang. Her heart sank at the idea of Winnie cancelling. The apartment felt vacant and enormous.

"Janet, dear?"

"Mother, how are you?"

"Fine. I was wondering if Winnie was there?"

"Yes, Mother, she's on her way." Janet noticed her irritation with Mother who always asked about someone else first when she called — Janet's brother or her daughter or even her ex-husband.

"Yes, I thought she might be. I've left several messages at the dormitory."

Janet waited. Ever since Mother had been laid off her job, she had been at loose ends, sometimes near the deep end. It was hard to know what to do for her.

"Janet, dear, do you have any plans today?"

"Well, yes, why?"

"I have to be over your way for a hearing test at the hospital and I wonder if we could have coffee — just the two of us."

"Sure." She agreed even though Mother had cancelled the last two weekend visits. She missed her job at the department store; her depression was immobilizing. "I mean I have to get Winnie settled at the computer and the Federal Express truck is coming. But sure, give me a ring when you're finished at the hospital."

"There's something I need to talk to you about. Something that's eating me up."

Janet worried. What had she done wrong? Nothing recently. But recently didn't matter. Mother still remembered that Janet had forgotten Mother's Day, 1960.

"I'd like to talk, just the two of us, privately."

The doorbell rang.

"Hang on a second . . ."

Winnie was more beautiful than ever. Elegantly tall, vivacious, intelligent. Janet had tried unsuccessfully to appreciate the spiked hairdo. Still, she was grateful Winnie hadn't shaved her head like her friends Wendy and Lisa. There was something magnificent about Winnie's combination of mauve hair and yellow sweater. Despite the vibrant colors, the girl looked exhausted.

"Jenny and I went to the city dancing last night. We paid a five dollar cover to get into a good club and the DJ was playing the wimpiest music. Jenny and I like soul. But he was in a time warp or something — playing Pink Floyd! Have you ever heard of anything so weird — oh, oops, I guess you have.

Anyway, we stayed there until two a.m. I'm really wiped."

"Have you had any breakfast?" Janet bit her tongue. She didn't have time to cook. Her accounts were a mess. Winnie had only asked to use the computer.

"Some pretzels on the ride over. You have anything?"

Janet smiled. "Still like five-minute eggs?"

Fixing breakfast for herself and Winnie, she relaxed. She caught a glimpse of herself in the dining-room mirror. What a railing she looked in her sweatshirt and jeans, a figure not much more maternal than Winnie's college friends. This face, though, had its share of wrinkles. Long, straight black hair also revealed her generation. Straight, she didn't like to think of herself as straight.

Winnie talked about her new classes and plans for Easter break. Then she said, "You know I'm kind of worried about Grandma."

"Yes?"

"Ever since they closed the store, she's been inviting me to spend time with her. Long periods of time. I went over last weekend for lunch. Then it turned into pinochle and a walk around the neighborhood."

Janet nodded.

"And her memory isn't so good. She forgot what game we were playing."

"Yes," Janet said, "I think she needs some kind of routine."

"That's it." Winnie gulped the coffee and pulled a face. "Better get going or I'll wind up unemployed like Grandma."

Janet followed her daughter into the study. "The disks are there. Do you know how to turn on the terminal?"

"Well, this is a little different from the one at school."

Janet's face fell as she looked away from her files.

"How do you center things?"

An hour later, Winnie was pecking through her resumé. Janet couldn't concentrate on her cancelled checks; all she could see was Winnie's vitae: Two years lifeguarding; six months waitressing; a year typing insurance forms. Her daughter had grown up. Janet glanced at the young woman squinting at the green screen. Yes, this was her daughter, the two-year-old protegé singing, "I love you, yeah, yeah, yeah," backed up by the Beatles in a tacky one-bedroom apartment in Bloomington twenty years ago. Yes, this was her daughter, the sweet punk who wanted to be a "financial analyst." This vocation was her father's doing. Since the divorce he had grown more and more conservative and probably introduced Winnie to the most unsavory assortment of stockbrokers and lawyers. Well, it was Winnie's life. After all, she, herself, was hardly the successful suburban matron her own mother hoped she had raised. You don't raise children any more than you raise chickens. You simply supply the feed and trust and they grow up. Janet returned to her books. Although she hated tax time, she was lucky to be making her living from her art. She was lucky in many ways.

"Mom, does this mean the end of the page? Is my resumé too long? Everyone says you have to get it on one page."

The phone rang.

"Oh, Mother," Janet sighed, "the Federal Express truck hasn't arrived yet. Let me see if Winnie can handle it . . . Yes, it's OK, Mother. I'll pick you up in five minutes."

Pulling out of the driveway, Janet noticed a truck striped in patriotic colors at the end of the street. At first she was puzzled that Federal Express would have another customer in her obscure neighborhood. She really should stop cultivating her eccentricity and learn more about the neighbors. She waited a moment to see if the truck were about to move. Ridiculous anxiety: a financial analyst was capable of handing a parcel to a truck driver. For some reason she suddenly recalled the girls exchanging valentines in her third grade class. Her favorite one was from Cindy, made with a border of real lace.

Mother stood, small and frail, in front of the hospital. Janet aimed for objectivity. Martha Frederickson was a handsome woman in her early seventies with grey hair and delicate features. She claimed her ground with the confidence of someone who had worked all her life and had raised two kids alone. As always she was wearing complementary muted colors, dark, low-heeled shoes and a matching handbag.

Janet honked and waved broadly, hoping for a smile. Martha looked lost. Janet summoned the strength to find her. The older woman nodded and laboriously climbed into the car. She began to talk immediately.

"I thought it was Thursday. The ear doctor's nurse called and said they had to change the appointment until one o'clock because they were running late. That was fine with me. They have a lot of patients. But I got here and realized that this was Friday, not Thursday. I'll just have to call and tell them I slept through the appointment. I don't like to lie, but it's the only thing I can do."

"Mother, just relax and put on your seat belt."

"Oh, yes, dear. I believe in seat belts."

Janet admired her mother's abiding faith in things technological despite a life of disappointment in the modern world.

When they turned onto Janet's street, the truck was idling in front of the apartment building. Had Winnie got confused? Had she, herself, filled out the form wrong? In an uncharacteristically daring automative maneuver, Janet pulled her car across the path of the truck and jumped out. The truck driver looked up, startled.

"My daughter was handling the package. Is everything OK?"

"Just fine, ma'am." The driver grinned down at her.

"Thank you." Janet smiled foolishly. It took all her

willpower not to instruct the driver to handle the package carefully.

A car honked from behind.

"You're blocking the road, dear," Martha called out the window, gripping her seat belt.

"Yes. Sorry." Janet waved to the car behind. She reversed into her own driveway.

Janet ran upstairs and stuck her head in the study, "Grandma's here, if you want to say hello."

Winnie smiled conspiratorially. "Just to say hello, OK? I really have to finish."

Janet paused in the kitchen doorway to admire her mother and daughter, joking with each other on the couch. Winnie really was a sweet young woman; Mother was coming alive. She was nervous about what Mother needed to discuss.

"Your brother makes a good cup of coffee too." Martha warmed her hands on the hot mug and talked about her son. He had invited her to New York the following month.

"That sounds nice," Janet encouraged. "You deserve a vacation." She thought about the St. Valentine's Day Massacre, wondering vaguely whether it had taken place in Chicago or New York.

"I'm afraid I have a long holiday ahead of me. Where would I find another job at my age . . .?"

"Mom. Mom." Winnie was shouting from the study. "Can you help me with the margins?"

Janet didn't want to desert Martha, just as she was embarking on her long vacation. "Here, did you see these pictures of Carmel? I keep meaning to put them in a photo album, but . . ."

"Organization was never your greatest skill," Martha smiled as she accepted the photographs.

Janet helped Winnie finish the resumé and showed her how to print it. She returned to the living-room to find her mother staring blankly out the window. What an old woman she looked today. Perhaps this was the consequence of being left alone for younger people with louder demands.

Winnie rushed in. "Are you sure this is going to reduce OK? I should have used the computer at school."

Martha regarded her granddaughter as if the girl were speaking Arabic.

Janet, caught between Winnie's anxiety and Mother's astonishment, sat down heavily on the chair and said she was sure everything would work out fine.

"Can I leave my books here while I go to the xerox shop?"

"Mi casa es su casa."

Martha concentrated on the photos, trying to match up images with people in the living-room.

As the door banged after Winnie, Janet realized she was starving.

"How about some lunch, Mother? I got crab to celebrate finishing my tapestry. There's plenty for two." She hoped, guiltily, that they would finish eating before Winnie returned from the copy shop. If you were stranded in the desert without enough food, would you feed your mother or your daughter first? She shook her head which contained a mind so often given to pointless ethical dilemmas.

The phone rang.

Janet switched on the answering machine to hear the accountant ask for her books which were now a week over-due. Janet turned down the volume and let her talk into the tape.

As she fixed the coffee, she mused about creating a robot to deal with Mother like her tape machine handled business. There were so many of Mother's needs she could not meet.

Finally seated in the front room, Janet could wait no longer. "Mother, Winnie may be back any time. While we have a minute to ourselves, will you tell me what you needed to talk about?"

Martha looked blank.

"Remember, on the phone you said you needed to talk about something that was 'eating you up'?"

"Oh," Martha frowned. "We've already discussed it, dear. In the car. The memory problem. It's quite frightening." She sounded reluctant to go into it again.

"Yes," Janet said softly, giving Martha time to continue if she wanted.

"While you were in the kitchen," Martha's voice grew stronger, "I was reading the newspaper here. An article about St. Valentine. Did you know that he was a Roman priest who ministered during the persecution of Claudius II. He was martyred under Aurelian, in 270."

"No." Janet smiled. "I didn't know that."

"Well, well." Martha turned to the door. "Look who's coming."

Winnie burst in, carrying a large stack of beige paper. "It went fine. The guy was really cute. He showed me how to center it. And he gave me a special deal. He said your computer had good contrast — that it was ideal for a resumé."

Janet hugged her daughter and felt unreasonably proud of her computer.

"I'll just get my binder." Winnie read her watch. "I may be able to do an hour at the library if I hurry."

Martha was staring into the coffee cup.

Winnie kissed her mother on the cheek. "Oh, Grandma, can I give you a lift to the bus-stop?"

Martha looked at Janet.

"No," Janet answered. "I'll take Grandma."

"OK." Winnie looked obliged. "Gotta rush. Bye, Mom. Bye, Grandma."

The door slammed on the suddenly small, stuffy flat. Martha was staring into her cup.

"I have to go shopping, Mother. Would you like to come with me — on the way to the bus?" She wanted to drive her mother all the way home, but knew even the offer would wound her pride.

"Yes." Martha perked up. "I'd love that. Remember when you were little and we used to go shopping?"

Afternoon was cast in the same heavy grey as the morning. Janet hated this waiting-room weather. San Francisco architecture had been drawn by people with sun in mind. On bright days, the white and yellow and pale blue houses reflected heat and light. But on cold, grim days the pastel edifices seemed to fade into oblivion. She longed for New York's tall brick buildings which resisted dreary weather, which seemed to impose character into grey days.

"I really like that little café."

"Which café, Mother?"

"You know, the one where we had pea soup, or was it lentil soup?"

"No, I don't remember. Where was it?"

"In the Mission. No, maybe not, maybe it was up on Union."

Janet was looking for a parking space, a pursuit which Mother, who did not drive, never took seriously.

"What are we shopping for?" Martha asked as they walked across the street.

"A Valentine's present."

They stopped at a window featuring bright red sweaters.

"Nice cardigan," Martha observed.

"Yes." Janet was delighted. "Let me get it for you for Valentine's Day."

"No." Martha shook her head vociferously. "I was thinking of you. Let me get it for you."

They walked on in search of Martha's favorite kind of dark chocolate. Finally, Janet found the right candy and a novel she thought her mother would enjoy.

The next shop had a sale on sweat-pants. Janet thought this might break through her laziness and get her to exercise class. "Mother, do you mind if I pop in here a second?"

The sweat-pants fit and as they left the shop Martha took Janet's arm. "Let me get them for you for Valentine's Day."

"OK." Janet smiled. They had been, after all, on sale. She noticed that her mother was flagging.

"How about some coffee?" Janet thought how young she felt when she was with Martha and how old she felt when she was with Winnie. What was her real age? Would Winnie be caught between her mother and daughter? Did financial analysts have daughters?

They sat in the café, reminiscing about family vacations. Next to them, an old woman left her purse on the table, wandering over to gossip with the cashier. Janet and Martha turned to each other in dismay. "Someone should tell her not to leave her purse." Janet heard her mother, or herself, say.

They finished their coffee in silence.

"Well, it's been a long day," sighed Martha. "I should be on my way."

"Sure, Mother." Janet was pleased by how much Martha had brightened over the afternoon. As they drove to the bus-stop she told herself that, once she got settled with retirement activities, everything would be fine. Briefly she considered how Mother had forgotten to pay for the sweat-pants. But she didn't want to bring it up, lest it revive her panic about memory.

"Do you mind if I take the novel *next* time? It's rather heavy to carry with all this."

"No." Janet shook her head, wishing she had insisted on the red sweater. Maybe Mother felt intimidated by the book. And she had always looked great in red.

It was dark by the time Janet arrived home. She wished daylight savings time functioned all year long. Carrying a cup of coffee into the study, she was heartened to see a red light pulsing on her answering machine. Two calls. She sat on the rug, sipped the coffee and listened. Oh, yes, the accountant asking about her late books. Winnie calling to say thanks and to wish her a Happy Valentine's Day.

Maybe she'd try on the sweat-pants and do some exercises to remove the kinks. Opening the bag, she found money scattered on top of the pants. Had she dropped her change in the bag like this? No, she counted fifty dollars; this wasn't her change. Of course, *Mother* had done this. Her Valentine. Janet slumped at her desk, surveying the money and the sweat-pants and the Federal Express receipt. She didn't know whether to laugh or cry. Just like that time in high school when she received a gorgeous red satin heart without a signature.

Best Quality

AMY TAN

Five months ago, after a crab dinner celebrating Chinese New Year, my mother gave me my "life's importance," a jade pendant on a gold chain. The pendant was not a piece of jewelry I would have chosen for myself. It was almost the size of my little finger, a mottled green and white color, intricately carved. To me, the whole effect looked wrong: too large, too green, too garishly ornate. I stuffed the necklace in my lacquer box and forgot about it.

But these days, I think about my life's importance. I wonder what it means, because my mother died three months ago, six days before my thirty-sixth birthday. And she's the only person I could have asked, to tell me about life's importance, to help me understand my grief.

I now wear that pendant every day. I think the carvings mean something, because shapes and details, which I never seem to notice until after they're pointed out to me, always mean something to Chinese people. I know I could ask Auntie Lindo, Auntie An-mei, or other Chinese friends, but I also know they would tell me a meaning that is different from what my mother intended. What if they tell me this curving line branching into three oval shapes is a pomegranate and that my mother was wishing me fertility and posterity? What if my mother really meant the carvings were a branch of pears to give me purity and honesty? Or ten-thousand-year droplets from the magic mountain, giving me my life's direction and a thousand years of fame and immortality?

And because I think about this all the time, I always notice other people wearing these same jade pendants — not the flat rectangular medallions or the round white ones with holes in the middle but ones like mine, a two-inch oblong of bright apple green. It's as though we were all sworn to the same secret covenant, so secret we don't even know what we belong to. Last weekend, for example, I saw a bartender wearing one. As I fingered mine, I asked him, "Where'd you get yours?"

"My mother gave it to me," he said.

I asked him why, which is a nosy question that only one Chinese person can ask another; in a crowd of Caucasians, two Chinese people are already like family.

"She gave it to me after I got divorced. I guess my mother's telling me I'm still worth something."

And I knew by the wonder in his voice that he had no idea what the pendant really meant.

At last year's Chinese New Year dinner, my mother had cooked eleven crabs, one crab for each person, plus an extra. She and I had bought them on Stockton Street in Chinatown. We had walked down the steep hill from my parents' flat, which was actually the first floor of a six-unit building they owned on Leavenworth near California. Their place was only six blocks from where I worked as a copywriter for a small ad agency, so two or three times a week I would drop by after work. My mother always had enough food to insist that I stay for dinner.

That year, Chinese New Year fell on a Thursday, so I got off work early to help my mother shop. My mother was seventy-one, but she still walked briskly along, her small body straight and purposeful, carrying a colorful flowery plastic bag. I dragged the metal shopping cart behind.

Every time I went with her to Chinatown, she pointed out other Chinese women her age. "Hong Kong ladies," she said, eyeing two finely dressed women in long, dark mink coats and perfect black hairdos. "Cantonese, village people," she whispered as we passed women in knitted caps, bent over in layers of padded tops and men's vests. And my mother — wearing light-blue polyester pants, a red sweater, and a child's green down jacket — she didn't look like anybody else. She had come here in 1949, at the end of a long journey that started in Kweilin in 1944; she had gone north to Chungking, where she met my father, and then they went southeast to Shanghai and fled farther south to Hong Kong, where the boat departed for San Francisco. My mother came from many different directions.

And now she was huffing complaints in rhythm to her walk downhill. "Even you don't want them, you stuck," she said. She was fuming again about the tenants who lived on the second floor. Two years ago, she had tried to evict them on the pretext that relatives from China were coming to live there. But the couple saw through her ruse to get around rent control. They said they wouldn't budge until she produced the relatives. And after that I had to listen to her recount every new injustice this couple inflicted on her.

My mother said the gray-haired man put too many bags in the garbage cans: "Cost me extra."

And the woman, a very elegant artist type with blond hair, had supposedly painted the apartment in terrible red and green colors. "Awful," moaned my mother. "And they take bath, two three times every day. Running the water, running, running, running, never stop!"

"Last week," she said, growing angrier at each step, "the *waigoren* accuse me." She referred to all Caucasians as *waigoren*, foreigners. "They say I put poison in a fish, kill that cat."

"What cat?" I asked, even though I knew exactly which one she was talking about. I had seen that cat many times. It was a big one-eared tom with gray stripes who had learned to jump on the outside sill of my mother's kitchen window. My mother would stand on her tiptoes and bang the kitchen window to scare the cat away. And the cat would stand his ground, hissing back in response to her shouts.

"That cat always raising his tail to put a stink on my door," complained my mother.

I once saw her chase him from her stairwell with a pot of boiling water. I was tempted to ask if she really had put poison in a fish, but I had learned never to take sides against my mother.

"So what happened to that cat?" I asked.

"That cat gone! Disappear!" She threw her hands in the air and smiled, looking pleased for a moment before the scowl came back. "And that man, he raise his hand like this, show me his ugly fist and call me worst Fukien landlady. I not from Fukien. Hunh! He knew nothing!" she said, satisfied she had put him in his place.

On Stockton Street, we wandered from one fish store to another, looking for the liveliest crabs.

"Don't get a dead one," warned my mother in Chinese. "Even a beggar won't eat a dead one."

I poked the crabs with a pencil to see how feisty they were. If a crab grabbed on, I lifted it out and into a plastic sack. I lifted one crab this way, only to find one of its legs had been clamped onto by another crab. In the brief tug-of-war, my

131

crab lost a limb.

"Put it back," whispered my mother. "A missing leg is a bad sign on Chinese New Year."

But a man in a white smock came up to us. He started talking loudly to my mother in Cantonese, and my mother, who spoke Cantonese so poorly it sounded just like her Mandarin, was talking loudly back, pointing to the crab and its missing leg. And after more sharp words, that crab and its leg were put into our sack.

"Doesn't matter," said my mother. "This number eleven, extra one."

Back home, my mother unwrapped the crabs from their newspaper liners and then dumped them into a sinkful of cold water. She brought out her old wooden board and cleaver, then chopped the ginger and scallions, and poured soy sauce and sesame oil into a shallow dish. The kitchen smelled of wet newspapers and Chinese fragrances.

Then, one by one, she grabbed the crabs by their back, hoisted them out of the sink and shook them dry and awake. The crabs flexed their legs in midair between sink and stove. She stacked the crabs in a multileveled steamer that sat over two burners on the stove, put a lid on top, and lit the burners. I couldn't bear to watch so I went into the dining room.

When I was eight, I had played with a crab my mother had brought home for my birthday dinner. I had poked it, and jumped back every time its claws reached out. And I determined that the crab and I had come to a great understanding when it finally heaved itself up and walked clear across the counter. But before I could even decide what to name my new pet, my mother had dropped it into a pot of cold water and placed it on the tall stove. I had watched with growing dread, as the water heated up and the pot began to clatter with this crab trying to tap his way out of his own hot soup. To this day, I remember that crab screaming as he thrust one bright red claw out over the side of the bubbling pot. It must have been my own voice, because now I know, of course, that crabs have no vocal cords. And I also try to convince myself that they don't have enough brains to know the difference between a hot bath and a slow death.

For our New Year celebration, my mother had invited her longtime friends Lindo and Tin Jong. Without even asking, my mother knew that meant including the Jongs' children: their son Vincent, who was thirty-eight years old and still living at home, and their daughter, Waverly, who was around my age. Vincent called to see if he could also bring his girlfriend, Lisa Lum. Waverly said she would bring her new fiancé, Rich Shields, who, like Waverly, was a tax attorney at Price Waterhouse. And she added that Shoshana, her four-year-old daughter from a previous marriage, wanted to know if my parents had a VCR so she could watch *Pinocchio,* just in case she got bored. My mother also reminded me to invite Mr. Chong, my old piano teacher, who still lived three blocks away at our old apartment.

Including my mother, father, and me, that made eleven people. But my mother had counted only ten, because to her way of thinking Shoshana was just a child and didn't count, at least not as far as crabs were concerned. She hadn't considered that Waverly might not think the same way.

When the platter of steaming crabs was passed around, Waverly was first and she picked the best crab, the brightest, the plumpest, and put it on her daughter's plate. And then she picked the next best for Rich and another good one for herself. And because she had learned this skill, of choosing the best, from her mother, it was only natural that her mother knew how to pick the next-best ones for her husband, her son, his girlfriend, and herself. And my mother, of course, considered the four remaining crabs and gave the one that looked the best to Old Chong, because he was nearly ninety and deserved that kind of respect, and then she picked another good one for my father. That left two on the platter: a large crab with a faded orange color, and number eleven, which had the torn-off leg.

My mother shook the platter in front of me. "Take it, already cold," said my mother.

I was not too fond of crab, ever since I saw my birthday crab boiled alive, but I knew I could not refuse. That's the way Chinese mothers show they love their children, not through hugs and kisses but with stern offerings of steamed dumplings, duck's gizzards, and crab.

I thought I was doing the right thing, taking the crab with the missing leg. But my mother cried, "No! No! Big one, you eat it. I cannot finish."

I remember the hungry sounds everybody else was making — cracking the shells, sucking the crab meat out, scraping out tidbits with the ends of chopsticks — and my mother's quiet plate. I was the only one who noticed her prying open the shell, sniffing the crab's body and then getting up to go to the kitchen, plate in hand. She returned, without the crab, but with more bowls of soy sauce, ginger, and scallions.

And then as stomachs filled, everybody started talking at once.

"Suyuan!" called Auntie Lindo to my mother. "Why you wear that color?" Auntie Lindo gestured with a crab leg to my mother's red sweater.

"How can you wear this color anymore! Too young!" she scolded.

My mother acted as though this were a compliment. "Emporium Capwell," she said. "Nineteen dollar. Cheaper than knit it myself."

Auntie Lindo nodded her head, as if the color were worth this price. And then she pointed her crab leg toward her future son-in-law, Rich, and said, "See how this one doesn't know how to eat Chinese food."

"Crab isn't Chinese," said Waverly in her complaining voice. It was amazing how Waverly still sounded the way she did twenty-five years ago, when we were ten and she had announced to me in that same voice, "You aren't a genius like me."

Auntie Lindo looked at her daughter with exasperation. "How do you know what is Chinese, what is not Chinese?" And then she turned to Rich and said with much authority, "Why you are not eating the best part?"

And I saw Rich smiling back, with amusement, and not humility, showing in his face. He had the same coloring as the crab on his plate: reddish hair, pale cream skin, and large dots of orange freckles. While he smirked, Auntie Lindo demonstrated the proper technique, poking her chopstick into the orange spongy part: "You have to dig in here, get this out. The brain is most tastiest, you try."

Waverly and Rich grimaced at each other, united in disgust. I heard Vincent and Lisa whisper to each other, "Gross," and then they snickered too.

Uncle Tin started laughing to himself, to let us know he also had a private joke. Judging by his preamble of snorts and leg slaps, I figured he must have practiced this joke many times: "I tell my daughter, Hey why be poor! Marry rich!" He laughed loudly and then nudged Lisa, who was sitting next to him. "Hey, don't you get it? Look what happen. She gonna marry this guy here. Rich. 'Cause I tell her to, *marry Rich.*"

"When *are* you guys getting married?" asked Vincent.

"I should ask you the same thing," said Waverly. Lisa looked embarrassed when Vincent ignored the question.

"Mom, I don't *like* crab!" whined Shoshana.

"Nice haircut," Waverly said to me from across the table.

"Thanks, David always does a great job."

"You mean you still go to that guy on Howard Street?" Waverly asked, arching one eyebrow. "Aren't you afraid?"

I could sense the danger, but I said it anyway: "What do you mean, afraid? He's always very good."

"I mean, he *is* gay," Waverly said. "He could have AIDS.

And he is cutting your hair, which is like cutting a living tissue. Maybe I'm being paranoid, being a mother, but you just can't be too safe these days. . . ."

And I sat there feeling as if my hair were coated with disease.

"You should go see my guy," said Waverly. "Mr. Rory. He does fabulous work, although he probably charges more than you're used to."

I felt like screaming. She could be so sneaky with her insults. Every time I asked her the simplest of tax questions, for example, she could turn the conversation around and make it seem as if I were too cheap to pay for her legal advice.

She'd say things like, "I really don't like to talk about important tax matters except in my office. I mean, what if you say something casual over lunch and I give you some casual advice. And then you follow it, and it's wrong because you didn't give me the full information. I'd feel terrible. And you would too, wouldn't you?"

At that crab dinner, I was so mad about what she said about my hair that I wanted to embarrass her, to reveal in front of everybody how petty she was. So I decided to confront her about the free-lance work I'd done for her firm, eight pages of brochure copy on its tax services. The firm was now more than thirty days late in paying my invoice.

"Maybe I could afford Mr. Rory's prices if someone's firm paid me on time," I said with a teasing grin. And I was pleased to see Waverly's reaction. She was genuinely flustered, speechless.

I couldn't resist rubbing it in: "I think it's pretty ironic that a big accounting firm can't even pay its own bills on time. I mean, really, Waverly, what kind of place are you working for?"

Her face was dark and quiet.

"Hey, hey, you girls, no more fighting!" said my father, as if Waverly and I were still children arguing over tricycles and crayon colors.

"That's right, we don't want to talk about this now," said Waverly quietly.

"So how do you think the Giants are going to do?" said Vincent, trying to be funny. Nobody laughed.

I wasn't about to let her slip away this time. "Well, every time I call you on the phone, you can't talk about it then either," I said.

Waverly looked at Rich, who shrugged his shoulders. She turned back to me and sighed.

"Listen, June, I don't know how to tell you this. That stuff you wrote, well, the firm decided it was unacceptable."

"You're lying. You said it was great."

Waverly sighed again. "I know I did. I didn't want to hurt your feelings. I was trying to see if we could fix it somehow. But it won't work."

And just like that, I was starting to flail, tossed without warning into deep water, drowning and desperate. "Most copy needs fine-tuning," I said. "It's . . . normal not to be perfect the first time. I should have explained the process better."

"June, I really don't think . . ."

"Rewrites are free. I'm just as concerned about making it perfect as you are."

Waverly acted as if she didn't even hear me. "I'm trying to convince them to at least pay you for some of your time. I know you put a lot of work into it. . . . I owe you at least that for even suggesting you do it."

"Just tell me what they want changed. I'll call you next week so we can go over it, line by line."

"June — I can't," Waverly said with cool finality. "It's just not . . . sophisticated. I'm sure what you write for your other clients is *wonderful*. But we're a big firm. We need somebody who understands that . . . our style." She said this touching her hand to her chest, as if she were referring to *her* style.

Then she laughed in a lighthearted way. "I mean, really, June." And then she started speaking in a deep television-announcer voice: "*Three* benefits, *three* needs, *three* reasons to buy . . . Satisfaction *guaranteed* . . . for today's and tomorrow's tax needs . . ."

She said this in such a funny way that everybody thought it was a good joke and laughed. And then, to make matters worse, I heard my mother saying to Waverly: "True, cannot teach style. June not sophisticate like you. Must be born this way."

I was surprised at myself, how humiliated I felt. I had been outsmarted by Waverly once again, and now betrayed by my own mother. I was smiling so hard my lower lip was twitching from the strain. I tried to find something else to concentrate on, and I remember picking up my plate, and then Mr. Chong's, as if I were clearing the table, and seeing so sharply through my tears the chips on the edges of these old plates, wondering why my mother didn't use the new set I had bought her five years ago.

The table was littered with crab carcasses. Waverly and Rich lit cigarettes and put a crab shell between them for an ashtray. Shoshana had wandered over to the piano and was banging notes out with a crab claw in each hand. Mr. Chong, who had grown totally deaf over the years, watched Shoshana and applauded: "Bravo! Bravo!" And except for his strange shouts, nobody said a word. My mother went to the kitchen and returned with a plate of oranges sliced into wedges. My father poked at the remnants of his crab. Vincent cleared his throat, twice, and then patted Lisa's hand.

It was Auntie Lindo who finally spoke: "Waverly, you let her try again. You make her do too fast first time. Of course she cannot get it right."

I could hear my mother eating an orange slice. She was the only person I knew who crunched oranges, making it sound as if she were eating crisp apples instead. The sound of it was worse than gnashing teeth.

"Good one take time," continued Auntie Lindo, nodding her head in agreement with herself.

"Put in lotta action," advised Uncle Tin. "Lotta action, boy, that's what I like. Hey, that's all you need, make it right."

"Probably not,' I said, and smiled before carrying the plates to the sink.

That was the night, in the kitchen, that I realized I was no better than who I was. I was a copywriter. I worked for a small ad agency. I promised every new client, "We can provide the sizzle for the meat." The sizzle always boiled down to "Three Benefits, Three Needs, Three Reasons to Buy." The meat was always coaxial cable, T-1 multiplexers, protocol converters, and the like. I was very good at what I did, succeeding at something small like that.

I turned on the water to wash the dishes. And I no longer felt angry at Waverly. I felt tired and foolish, as if I had been running to escape someone chasing me, only to look behind and discover there was no one there.

I picked up my mother's plate, the one she had carried into the kitchen at the start of the dinner. The crab was untouched. I lifted the shell and smelled the crab. Maybe it was because I didn't like crab in the first place. I couldn't tell what was wrong with it.

After everybody left, my mother joined me in the kitchen. I was putting dishes away. She put water on for more tea and sat down at the small kitchen table. I waited for her to chastise me.

"Good dinner, Ma," I said politely.

"Not so good," she said, jabbing at her mouth with a toothpick.

"What happened to your crab? Why'd you throw it away?"

"Not so good," she said again. "That crab die. Even a beggar don't want it."

"How could you tell? I didn't smell anything wrong."

"Can tell even before cook!" She was standing now, looking out the kitchen window into the night. "I shake that crab before cook. His legs — droopy. His mouth — wide open, already like a dead person."

"Why'd you cook it if you knew it was already dead?"

"I thought . . . maybe only just die. Maybe taste not too bad. But I can smell, dead taste, not firm."

"What if someone else had picked that crab?"

My mother looked at me and smiled. "Only *you* pick that crab. Nobody else take it. I already know this. Everybody else want best quality. You thinking different."

She said it in a way as if this were proof — proof of something good. She always said things that didn't make any sense, that sounded both good and bad at the same time.

I was putting away the last of the chipped plates and then I remembered something else. "Ma, why don't you ever use those new dishes I bought you? If you didn't like them, you should have told me. I could have changed the pattern."

"Of course, I like," she said, irritated. "Sometime I think something is so good, I want to save it. Then I forget I save it."

And then, as if she had just now remembered, she unhooked the clasp of her gold necklace and took it off, wadding the chain and the jade pendant in her palm. She grabbed my hand and put the necklace in my palm, then shut my fingers around it.

"No, Ma," I protested. "I can't take this."

"Nala, nala" — Take it, take it — she said, as if she were scolding me. And then she continued in Chinese. "For a long time, I wanted to give you this necklace. See, I wore this on my skin, so when you put it on your skin, then you know my meaning. This is your life's importance."

I looked at the necklace, the pendant with the light green jade. I wanted to give it back. I didn't want to accept it. And yet I also felt as if I had already swallowed it.

"You're giving this to me only because of what happened tonight," I finally said.

"What happen?"

"What Waverly said. What everybody said."

"Tss! Why you listen to her? Why you want to follow behind her, chasing her words? She is like this crab." My mother poked a shell in the garbage can. "Always walking sideways, moving crooked. You can make your legs go the other way."

I put the necklace on. It felt cool.

"Not so good, this jade," she said matter-of-factly, touching the pendant, and then she added in Chinese: "This is young jade. It is a very light color now, but if you wear it every day it will become more green."

My father hasn't eaten well since my mother died. So I am here, in the kitchen, to cook him dinner. I'm slicing tofu. I've decided to make him a spicy bean-curd dish. My mother used to tell me how hot things restore the spirit and health. But I'm making this mostly because I know my father loves this dish and I know how to cook it. I like the smell of it: ginger, scallions, and a red chili sauce that tickles my nose the minute I open the jar.

Above me, I hear the old pipes shake into action with a *thunk!* and then the water running in my sink dwindles to a trickle. One of the tenants upstairs must be taking a shower. I remember my mother complaining: "Even you don't want them, you stuck." And now I know what she meant.

As I rinse the tofu in the sink, I am startled by a dark mass that appears suddenly at the window. It's the one-eared tomcat from upstairs. He's balancing on the sill, rubbing his flank against the window.

My mother didn't kill that damn cat after all, and I'm relieved. And then I see this cat rubbing more vigorously on the window and he starts to raise his tail.

"Get away from there!" I shout, and slap my hand on the window three times. But the cat just narrows his eyes, flattens his one ear, and hisses back at me.

Pageant

S. L. WISENBERG

Ceci Rubin's mother has driven her from Houston to San Antonio for a talent show. It is a Saturday. Usually Ceci spends her weekends at charm school classes for little girls at Neiman's and acting lessons at the Alley Theater's children's school. When she misses class for a contest, she makes up the work on weeknights. Her mother helps her with this juggling and preparing — she is Ceci's "aide de crimp," her father once said, and Ceci parrots the phrase. Her mother has helped her, for example, incorporate her eyeglasses into her act. She has learned to remove them and gesture at appropriate spots, so that now they seem necessary to her performance — "absolutely indispensable," as Ceci puts it. It is 11:30 and they have just arrived at the parking lot of San Antonio High School. The humid air disappoints — her mother had promised it would be dry, after all they were going west, even if it was along a river. She fears her curls will turn to frizz.

In the middle of the stage of the Davy Crockett Auditorium, Ceci does her act—her little elocution, Kay Thompson's "Eloise." ("I am Eloise. I am six. I am a city child. I live at the Plaza. . . .") Though Ceci has never been to New York, her idea of New York is so strong that it wouldn't matter if New York were mythical. The Manhattan of her Eloise piece is the same larger-than-life place that drew Dorothy Parker and James Thurber and in the very same tradition, Garrison Keillor. She does not know of Garrison Keillor yet. No one does. Ceci is eight and pouty-lipped and does not yet have the feeling: Who are you to thrust yourself in the public eye? She is judged a finalist but she does not win. She is in the top four. She has come to expect this. She hardly ever wins. When she does, she is confounded, does not know how to react. Grace does not come naturally to her.

Her grandparents have driven in from Austin. They have brought flowers. She has always wanted roses, white roses. She thinks roses are elegant. Grandma and Grandpa have brought her purple irises from the garden. They are wrapped in paper towels and foil. They have held them throughout the performance, or maybe left them sitting on the chair. The edge of one petal is wet and crinkled and dark like lettuce gets when it's handled too much. It is ruined. They have brought her garden flowers ruined by their lack of care. And she has lost. "The judges did not understand," says her mother, "they are too Texan." Her mother is trying to thank her parents for Ceci. For coming out. Ceci does not thank them. She wants them to take her to an elegant French restaurant (like Eloise, she imagines, goes to) and if they cannot buy her a whole bouquet, she wants one perfect white rose at her place, next to the dinner napkin rolled in its silver holder. She wants them to ask her opinion of the dumb singer from Kerrville and her "Nearer My God to Thee." Ceci is eight but she has heard about the separation of church and state. Her father talks about it. He has explained it to her. She wants to know if the girl can be arrested for singing about a Christian God in front of all of them, this Saturday afternoon of Ceci's sabbath, when her grandparents usually go to services and eat herring and kichel and talk to their friends. She has seen her grandfather pray. He stands and makes a great noise. It is embarrassing. He vibrates like the windup organ grinder and monkey Ceci has at home. She does not know these people, her mother's parents, well at all. Sometimes she feels she is an orphan. She has imagined the orphanage she came from, a place like Madeleine lives with Miss Clavel. Her mother gives her a slight shove, says, "Thank your grandparents for the flowers." She wants to kick them. She wants to wake them up from thinking she is merely an eight-year-old produced by their daughter and son-in-law Ruben, a little girl who does not understand life. She understands life. She talks to God. She talks to her dog. She understands the pain of asthma. She has been to deep places but she cannot begin to find the words to tell them this. She too wonders about suffering. She has read the diary of Anne Frank, slowly, carefully, because the style is too old for her. Like the dresses she sometimes wears. When she dresses up she looks like she's going to a job interview.

She is very young. She is only now learning how to write in cursive. The other children make fun of her special trips but are awed at the prizes and clippings she brings to Show and Tell. (She is still that young, to have a Show and Tell.) They are standing here forever, these three generations, between the first row and the stage, and all around, other families are talking, the shurring and hissing that has become so familiar — the crying of the poor losers, sore losers — and the smell of sweat mixed with the sticky fragrances of the sponsors: sulphury hair perm, strawberry perfume for girls, ubiquitous cloying junior hairspray. The sweet sure smell of red lipstick. (White lipstick smells differently, more waxy, more like chocolate.) The crayon smell of the eyebrow pencil. Ceci's mother doesn't let her wear more than a dash of eyebrow pencil under and along her eyelashes, but other girls wear layers of mascara, acres of it, false eyelashes, even, glittery eyeshadow. Sometimes she borrows blue-violet eyeshadow from a girl from Bastrop who shows up at all the same competitions, and she puts a dab on the corner of her eyes. It is the color of the irises. Her grandparents are impatient. They are more disappointed than she is. They want a cuddly granddaughter who is cute and kewpie-lipped and who wows the judges and here they have this sullen unappreciative thing who didn't even win a ribbon. (Just missed it by one.) Who wants to be consulted on theological matters, though they do not know this. She cannot tell them, cannot tell them how she spends time wondering if Joseph in the Bible — that is what she calls him, out of some sort of respect, Joseph-in-the-Bible — brought his fate upon himself. She feels a kinship with him, feels his joy at the flamboyant coat, his pain in the pit, alone, such fear, such casting out. She doesn't tell them any of this. Years later, she imagines them saying, "Why didn't you tell us what you were feeling?" And she imagines answering, accusing, "Why didn't you?" But by the time there is peace, it is too late, they have grown feeble, and when she is in her twenties, when she asks her grandmother questions, the older woman recoils: "Why do you come here and ask and ask?"

But back then, time is stretching out and they are standing there forever and Ceci is silent. Her grandmother with her cracky voice (it has been that way for years and years, forever) says, "Well, Ceci, it's not the end of the world, we thought you did very well," and she hears the patronizing in her grandmother's voice, though she doesn't have that word yet. She hears the separation, what lies beneath it: *I am old and know much and you are my daughter's child, two generations removed, you will never know what we do,* and she hears in that voice, *You are not as good as we are,* and the tragedy of the misunderstanding grips her, though she does not know this is what it is. They do not understand, the judges do not understand, and for the first time Ceci becomes dissatisfied with Eloise, because Eloise cannot help her now — this flimsy Eloise, this Curious George in skirts, who cannot look at the deeper questions, who cannot lead her to words that reach to souls and grab them and wrench them from their lack of concentration. Ceci does not realize it then but she wants to be the rabbi, she wants to stand up there and not amuse and not show the judges the magical New York that she imagines (for the first time that is not enough, to impose her vision, because she is afraid they do not take it in, they let it wash over them, hear only the chirping of her voice), but get at something more important, that she can only guess at then. She wants to change them, fundamentally, make a difference in their lives. But she knows only a glimmer of this. All she knows is she does not want these irises-picked-from-the-yard because they don't make her feel special enough and she wants to shock them with her erudition or her melodrama but cannot. *I am not who you think I am.* She is only half their size and dressed the way her mother and she assumes that a Manhattan girl from another era would dress: white flat straw hat, black tights, navy dress with hip-level sash. She will bite her mother's parents if they say she looks cute.

She doesn't answer them. She feels badness swelling inside her. She doesn't want their damn flowers. She flails for words. She is frightened of saying this word in front of them. She takes the flowers and drops them and for a moment she still has a chance — she could pick them up, say the minimum: "Thank you" or "Sorry." But she doesn't. She won't. If they were to take her to the guillotine she would not say them. Guillotine is a word she does know.

A beat. She steps on them — she steps on their purple loving-hands-from-home irises. She grinds them with the toes and heels of both of her dull black soft leather Mary

Janes. Her grandmother flutters: "Oh Cecilia, you're just disappointed in losing. You still deserve flowers." She moves to pat her head. But Ceci's mother knows better. Ceci's mother knows of her badness. She wants to leach it, beat it from her daughter. She grabs Ceci's arm, and a feeling of danger that is almost sexual, that is sexual, rises in Ceci. She knows what her mother will do — she fears, she hates her mother and everyone else at this moment. Ceci the Stuckup Snob (as they call her at these contests, a few of the girls, just a few) will get her comeuppance in front of the little girls who cry when they lose, Ceci who never cries in front of anyone for any reason, who says, "I don't care so much, I do it for the experience." Ceci's mother is grabbing her, in anger, in her shame before her own parents, shame that she has raised her daughter wrong, has made all the wrong decisions, ended up with the wrong family, a family that is not the way she wants it to be. Her husband Ruben who makes bubblebath for the fun of the nation, so he says, yet is too tired to bring joy to her life, has not danced with her, for example, since their own wedding; her other daughter, who is not in contests, stays home quietly and does not act up but instead of being good is just mediocre. Ceci's grandparents accuse Ceci's mother of pushing her, Ceci has heard them say that, and once they even ventured to say she could be causing her daughter's asthma. Now Ceci's mother has wrenched her across her lap and the mother's frustration pounds into the daughter, into her body, sharp surprise cracks of pain real pain that should not be surprises, she expects them, maybe she even deserves them. They sting, they pop and all she can feel is she hates her she hates her, she wants her to die. Ceci knows she can either lie here face down, and be perfectly still, like a European martyr, like a Jew in the camps, or she can rage and scream, as she is doing, though she knows it only fuels her mother's anger and will make her attack go on forever, in reaction to Ceci's pink-painted fingernails digging into her calves, bodies locked in battle, ferocity that can't let up, for how can they stop, for then they will have to face one another?

It is finally her grandfather who tears them apart. Reproach fills his face, but no one dares lift her face to read it.

Ceci cannot imagine she will ride back four hours with this woman who wants to kill something out of her, this woman who has grabbed her in sincere supreme effort to hurt her, her flesh and blood, to cause pain and beat into her the rhythm of her own shame. Ceci runs through a doorway back to the school gym just down the hall. Each of the girls had been assigned a locker there. She undresses in the shower stall so no one will see as she sheds her underwear. She turns, while the water is running, touching the redness of her bottom, the way her sister showed her with sunburn: touch it, turns white, lift finger, turns red again. She stays under the shower forever it seems, the water running hot and strong over her sticky hairsprayed hair and down to her bottom, where it stings and she soaps it over and over and listens in awe to the depth of her own sobbing, gasping into hiccups, her lungs still clear, and then starts to sing, to replace the wordless breaths, a mix of everything — "Hatikava," "Dead Man's Curve," "Go Away, Little Girl," "David Melech Yisrael," and finally turns off the water, fascinated by the white wrinkles of her fingers, almost transparent on the tips. She imagines they will never be restored to smoothness.

In the car Ceci gets in the backseat, to punish her mother, saying she wants to stretch out and sleep. Her mother plays talk radio, switching from town to town. The same news, different voices. At home Ceci does not, as she usually does, go running to her father.

Time passes. Ceci enters more competitions. But she is changed. She looks for serious parts and is named a finalist fewer and fewer times. "Whatever can that girl's mother be thinking of?" the judges wonder. Sometimes the judges do take a liking to her, the very few who actually enjoy the idea of a nine- or ten-year-old reciting the memoirs of Eleanor Roosevelt and Helen Keller. But Ceci's career in the talent circuit quickly winds down.

Later she will mark that afternoon in San Antonio High as not the end of her childhood or of anything hallowed like innocence but the day she realized that no one understood her, no one would ever understand her, the day she felt her heart begin to close. As years went by, even as she refused to confide in him out of a sense of loyalty to her mother, whose disappointment she sensed and somehow took as her own fate, Ceci wanted more and more to become her father Ruben — safe in his office with consumer surveys and marketing plans, reports of chemical analyses and European break- throughs, where nothing of this life could touch him.

Baby Houston
(an excerpt)

JUNE ARNOLD

Hallie must have gotten pregnant on her honeymoon — but why wait, in my opinion; if you know you want children you might as well go on and have them and Hallie is already twenty-three.

She found an apartment two blocks from Main Street near downtown — the entire upper story of a ramshackle old house. We are sitting in the room at the top of the steps, which we call the living room. On the floor she has a galvanized washtub holding a cake of ice; behind it an electric fan is blowing in our direction. Outside the temperature is ninety-eight. I am thankful that I am not pregnant.

Hallie's ankles are the size of her calves and her feet won't fit into any shoes. She is describing the colors she plans to use to paint the apartment for Dora. Neither of us has the slightest doubt that it will be Dora.

She looks so misshapen and miserable that I send my mind back to the day a few months ago when I was buying her trousseau. We were in Semaan's looking for the bridal nightgown and robe set. Semaan's dressing room is huge with gilt chairs and two walls of mirrors, and the scent of something like Chanel No. 5 is filling the store.

I almost could not bear the beauty of Hallie's body. Her skin had the luster of pink pearls, particularly over her high plump breasts (which are now huge and rest on an equally protruding belly). My throat was dry but I smoked several Chesterfields anyway to quiet an intense nervousness: I felt that I had been dumped into the myth of Ceres: I was Ceres and this perfect golden grain of prime wheat was my Persephone about to be seized and dragged off to the underworld.

Through the Chanel No. 5 I could smell Hallie's insistent personal scent, which was like fresh spring air in a wheat field, a smell she has carried in her pores since babyhood, through horse sweat and adolescent glands and young adult experiments with lemon soap, a smell that has only become more definite with age just as her eyes have decided to be finally green.

She had a beautiful bust like the marble of Aphrodite — I remembered Cad telling me that if I can say breast of chicken I can say breast of girl, and smiled.

"What?" Hallie said.

"Nothing," I said. "I was just thinking what a beautiful figure you have."

I didn't remember that her body was so finished before; she had filled out in the two years she'd been away — she looked womanly, ripe and mature as a luscious camellia. I was sorry I was staring and searched for another cigarette, took out my comb instead. I wanted to comb her hair.

She said, "This is just the most beautiful thing I have ever seen in my whole life." It was a silk nightgown in the indescribably vibrant cream-white of a magnolia blossom with fine lace along the neckline and armholes; the matching peignoir had a round collar and tied at the throat and made her look like a fairytale princess for the first time in her life that I could remember. "I don't deserve anything anywhere near this royal. It's magical. I just . . ." Her eyes were profoundly grateful — not, I thought, because I was ready to buy it for her but primarily because I announced that she deserved it by bringing her here. "I feel like you in it," she said.

"Can I refill your iced tea?"

Her voice shakes me out of my heat trance and I get up. "Let me get it. I hate to see you walking on those poor feet." I wonder if Hallie will survive until the first of November. Because she is normally so small she looks enormous already; tall women don't appear to get as big.

"Maybe Dora will come early."

I hand her a refilled glass of iced tea in which the ice is already melting. "I wish she'd be born on my birthday. I can't think of a more exciting present for my half-century day."

Hallie laughs. "Now you heard that, Dora," she says to her belly. "Mother wants a birthday present."

"Are you sure you want to name her Dora?" I am immensely pleased, of course; I just want to hear it again. She already said she wouldn't name her Eudora, just Dora — so no one could give her a nickname.

"She's already named."

"Well, I'm going to get her grandmother's house ready for her."

As soon as Hallie got pregnant I began to imagine my granddaughter and I was certain my old house was not a grandmother's house. It is too close to the street for one thing, and on the street all the time, except on rare bad-weather days, there are teenagers and children asserting their youth. It is time for me to live in a stately neighborhood where children only visit — in fact, I am tired of hearing half-grown noises altogether. I want to be surrounded by the cheeps of birds and the gurgles of my baby granddaughter.

"Sister's is the only house in Houston beautiful enough for Dora," I say. "My old house is just a party house which people don't look at. But a baby would look. I certainly don't want a house that could twist her esthetic sense all out of kilter, now do I? Isn't it true that taste is set forever while their eyes still have cornea color spilling over into the whites?"

"Maybe even earlier. Maybe if I start painting the apartment now she'll grow up to be a house painter."

"An artist."

"An interior decorator."

"I hope she never grows up at all!" I've got to go. I'm meeting Sis at Semaan's to pick out Dora's christening dress. I stand up.

"Will you be in Auntie's — your new house by your birthday?"

"We'll be in the streets. We have to be out of the Overbrook in a month and Sis won't leave her house until her roses have stopped blooming. She thinks I'll let them all die." I want to leave quickly — it hurts me to see her standing on those feet. Although her ankles and feet are enormous they look more like jellyfish than supports.

"Well, take your choice," Hallie says, her voice so happy it is clearly unaware of her lower limbs. "What's it to be: a birthday present or a house-warming present? You can't have both."

"Mugwumps." I kiss her forehead, careful not to throw her off balance. "You let her take her time. We want her to be perfect."

"She'll be perfect."

The Teapot

CHRISTIAN MCEWEN

I am talking to the teapot. We are being nice to each other as hard as we can. It isn't something we've had much time to practice. There are certain topics we avoid: ourselves, for instance, and our pasts, and where they overlap. But there are other subjects: the husband and father, for example. He comes up quite frequently.

"Do you remember," says the teapot, settling herself comfortably on the table by the fire. "You do remember, don't you —" and I pretend to listen.

But really I am looking at the teapot herself, her brown and glistening sides, the sturdy, happy way she pours the tea.

"How's that?" she asks me.

"Great," I tell her. "Great." And I sit back in my chair and sip the tea. The room is crowded with furniture: desks and bookcases, two chests-of-drawers, a bureau, and a big four-poster bed. Everywhere I look I see tokens of the teapot's other lives.

"She hasn't thrown anything away," I say to myself. "Nothing at all."

Between the bureau and the bed, there is a wooden chest, and on this several objects are laid out, as if for a display. There is a catechism with the teapot's name in front, a lacy Victorian valentine, a blue cloak and a tall vase of flowers. There is even an old list of things to do.

I pick up the list and read it over to myself. *Chapel flowers,* it says. *Scottish Horticultural Society. Children's dentist. Cheese.*

"Cheese," I repeat aloud. "What kind of cheese?"

"Edam," says the teapot unexpectedly. "Yes," she adds, as if continuing a conversation. "I wanted you to see those things." And then she hums a little, to distract us both, and asks me please to do the washing up, because the priest is coming over.

Once there was a teapot, small and sweet, a nutbrown maiden on a dainty tray. This teapot is a stubborn matron with a mind of her own. I run the water for the washing up, and I am little, shriveled, monkey-hunched, a toy reflection in her glistening sides.

"Stop dreaming," says the teapot. "Or you'll never get it done. The fairy liquid's on the shelf up there."

It is dusk already, and the priest has been and gone. The teapot is sitting on the rug beside the fireplace. "Do you remember," she continues, "how the husband and father used to sit here in the evening, one leg hooked over the other, and the patched sole showing?"

"Yes," I nod. I remember the husband and father in all sorts of places and in all sorts of ways. At teatime I remember him with a cup of tea and two glasses next to his plate. There is one glass of whiskey, and there is one glass of milk.

"Ah," says the teapot, and I can see she is thinking of the

life of the valentine.

It is a pretty Victorian valentine, with a Cock Robin and a Jenny Wren singing to each other on a flowering branch. There is no inscription, but when I open the card a scent of lavender wafts out of it, lavender and rose geranium. "It *is* nice, isn't it?" the teapot says. She is remembering her dancing days, the polished floors of strange enormous ball-rooms stretching off under her downcast eyes, and the husband and father hovering in the distance, waiting.

> *It was the nightingale, and not the lark*
> *That pierc'd the fearful hollow of thine ear —*
> *Believe me, love, it was the nightingale.*

There is yearning in her voice, and a kind of exultation, and as I watch the brown pot disappears. This is a different, lither creature, shy and fervent. "No," she whispers. "No, I couldn't do it." And then softly, unmistakably, "Yes."

I see her, and I see beyond her, to a small serious girl with that same hooded gaze, that same beauty. I don't need to fetch the catechism or the copy of *Romeo and Juliet* to know which passages are marked. Besides, the teapot doesn't look as if she cares. She has left the rug and is rocking back and forth on the brick edge of the fireplace, muttering to herself snatches from Saint Paul. "And there are three virtues, faith, hope and charity, and the greatest of these is charity."

"Cold as charity," I say involuntarily, and the teapot stops her rocking. "Yes," she answers, "and I wish it were not so. But I couldn't help it. I didn't have the experience. You know that. The life of the catechism is a simple life. Juliet, anyone can be Juliet. And who would turn from the pleasures of a valentine? But the other things, you see, I had to learn. He asked so much of me, sometimes." Again she is silent, thinking of the husband and father, and I am silent too. I can feel the dregs of the tea turning inside her. "What do you think," she asks suddenly, "of the vase of flowers?"

I bite my lips, because of all the objects on display, the one I like least is the vase of flowers.

It is true that it is very carefully arranged. And it looks wonderful at a distance. But it is a thing to be seen in perspective: at the top of the stairs, maybe, or across a hall. Close to, the water smells a little stale, and the flower-heads are oddly disproportionate.

I pause a moment, wondering what to say.

"It is cool," I tell her. "It is beautifully arranged. But you know I've always seen it from a long way off. And somehow when I look at it, I hear the snip of secateurs, and a Mozart record — on the second side. I see the husband and father, and the vase of flowers behind him, reflecting him in all his glory."

"Glory?" asks the teapot. "You said glory?"

I would answer, but she doesn't give me time. Again, her mood has altered. She is thinking of the list of things to do.

"You couldn't know," she says. "You've never lived like that. I can't expect that you would understand. But everything, I knew *everything*. How many spoons there were in that drawer over there, who was coming to lunch next Saturday. My mind was ordered to a terrifying degree. I was ravaged by detail."

She looks up, and the flames dance along the edge of her nose. "Where is that list?" she asks me. "Have you seen it?"

I fetch the list for her, and lay it on the rug. She reads it slowly, as if it were written in a foreign language. "Thirteenth of April, let me see. Of course, yes, I remember. Mass at eight o'clock. Breakfast with the priest. Letters and telephone calls, early elevenses. A party of Americans to take around the garden. The little ones to go to Edinburgh —"

I look over her shoulder at the clear italic handwriting. 13.iv.78. "I always liked the way you did the months in Roman numerals."

"I liked that too," says the teapot. She smiles, and looks into the fire. "You're right, you're right. It's silly to get angry. There were always the little pleasures."

I bow my head, overcome by the memory of the teapot's pleasures. I remember the husband and father scowling as he prepared her breakfast tray. Muesli and milk, honey for the tea. "How can she bear it?" he demanded. "Every day the same."

Monotony, he called it. But the teapot was glad of a little monotony. The husband and father was unpredictable enough for both of them. She liked, she said, for things to be reliable. Each night she drew her glazed chintz curtains shut. And every morning she opened them onto the same view.

"And so I lived those years," the teapot says. "And so I managed."

"You did more than that," I tell her. "Much much more. Have you forgotten the blue cloak?"

"No," says the teapot. "I have not forgotten." She doesn't want to talk about the blue cloak. She thinks I will criticize her. She has had dealings with me for a long time now, and she believes I judge her. This is true. I judge her fiercely, as all children judge their parents. But that is not my purpose here.

"I want to understand," I say, and mean it.

The teapot stares at me. She does not speak. Then, "Shut your eyes," she says. "Just shut your eyes."

It isn't easy, but I do as I am told. For a long moment I see the teapot's nose, and a kind of wink that comes from a trick in the glaze. Then I see a woman sitting up in bed, feeding her baby son. Her right breast is exposed. Through the walls come the voices of the nuns.

"My child," they say. "It is a lovely mother you have. The perfect Catholic mother."

I watch my mother, my personal virgin, from the great

distance at the bottom of the bed. "Dear Mama," I write. "Thank you for the cherry nougat. It was very good. How is the hamster and Tony Owl? Lots of love. P.S. Can you send me some more stamps?"

The Virgin Mother does not tell us fairy stories in case we think God is a fairy story. She gives us missals with our names in front, and holy pictures and special rosaries. She sits on the sofa in the nursery and hears our prayers. "I didn't believe in God," my brother tells her later. "I thought I was praying to you."

I pray to the Virgin Mother to take me away from school, but she does not listen. She picks flowers, she polishes the silver candlesticks. "Look," I tell her. "Look, my knee is bleeding."

The Virgin Mother is fond of blood. She goes to the bathroom cupboard and gets the First Aid kit. She cleans the wound, and puts a bandage on, with careful strips of plaster. "You are brave," she tells me. And then she goes away.

"You are frowning," says the teapot. "Why do you frown?"

"Because I hate all that," I tell her. "And it doesn't help."

"What would help?" the teapot asks me, and at once I am repentant.

"You did — lots of times."

I remember coming in out of the snow, all of us quarreling and noisy. I remember the husband and father slumped in his chair. And I remember the teapot, with her girlish profile, her handle arching welcoming towards me.

"Hey teapot," I say suddenly. I am so unceremonious I can't believe it. But the teapot sputters as if I'd given her a great compliment. I warm my fingers on her shiny sides.

Corsage

MAUREEN BRADY

Leslie woke but stayed in bed, eyes closed, waiting for the alarm. The morning light was so bright it blasted right through her eyelids. Though she prized having the bed by the window, this day the sun was too penetrating. It made her feel edgy, as if she were being watched, though Melissa seemed still to be sleeping.

Her stomach was full of fear overturned on top of excitement, the same as it had been the day before when she'd gotten the note from the principal's office. She'd been in Algebra, sleepy both from lunch and from the drone in Mr. Jones' voice as he worked toward solving the problem on the board. Her sleepiness had contributed to how it had seemed unreal when the student assistant came in and handed her the folded piece of paper. She had never been the sort to get messages in school. Mindy Roberts had got one when her brother shot himself. She'd seen other kids get them, then follow the messenger out of the room, and she never knew what'd happened to them, though she'd kept her ears open, hoping to hear. She read the note to see if she had to leave the room. It said she was one of the top five students in her junior high graduating class and she would receive an award for this in assembly the next day. She stuck it haphazardly in the back of her notebook and zeroed back in on the algebra problem. She thought she might have misread the note. Or perhaps she'd read it right, but it had been mistakenly delivered to the wrong person.

Shelby caught her racing out when the bell rang and asked, "What's the matter?"

"Nothing," Leslie said, then, "Wait, I'll show you." She leafed through the back pages of her notebook, worrying she'd lost the note already, but found it and watched as Shelby read it.

"Hey, this is great," Shelby said. "I guess I should be proud to be your friend."

"I guess so," Leslie said, flashing a quick smile.

"I always knew you were a brain," Shelby said triumphantly.

In the dark of the toilet stall in the girl's room, Leslie let Shelby's pride billow out in her chest. Wow. She was secretly impressed. She'd always been a good student but quiet about it, no trouble to the teachers. A good half of her motivation was to never stand out as someone who didn't know the answer. The other half was how she'd discovered learning was like the window over her bed, a place to see out.

The alarm rang, and Melissa sprang into the day. Leslie pulled the sheet over her face until Melissa had gone into the bathroom, then inched herself out of bed and checked herself in the mirror. Strange how normal she looked even when she was nearly paralyzed with panic. How was she going to make it up those stairs and across the stage without tripping all over the place? One thing that calmed her: Melissa wouldn't be there. Melissa was in high school.

Leslie stared with dread into her closet, her body impatient with the discomfort she predicted feeling in most any of her clothes. What she had worn to bed was what she liked best — a football jersey, bright red with white letters across the chest and back: number 14. Though loose on her shoulders, it made them look square, even dropped slightly forward the way she liked to hold them. "Shoulders back, chest forward, don't be ashamed of your bosom," her mother was always saying. She wasn't ashamed of her bosom. She was ashamed of her mother's archaic way of describing it. She had two little blooms growing on her chest and she didn't always feel like showing them to the world. She liked to sometimes keep new changes to herself.

She studied herself in the mirror again. Her hips were slim. She stood in an angular pose, all her weight on one foot, so the jersey hung on her hip and showed her form. She put her hand on the other hip. Tough. It made her look like someone who knew what she was doing. Her face was too easy; it didn't match her body. It showed fear. It showed the little girl she hadn't been able to grow out of yet. She had a lot of freckles, which she considered childish. She thought she could like herself better with a different kind of skin. She wished she could get a good suntan so she could blush without being noticed, but if she stayed out too long, she only got a burn.

She wished she were a boy so she could wear pants to the assembly. She'd be less vulnerable. So many things could happen to you in a skirt. You could get your period and have blood run down your legs before you knew it. You could fall and have your underpants show. Engrossed in your own thinking, you could sit wrong and be called loose. You could get it wrinkled on your bicycle and not know how the back looked until someone tapped your shoulder and told you, and even then there was nothing you could do about it.

She went back to the closet and began a second shuffle through her clothes, desperation growing. Okay, she preached to herself, you *have* nothing perfect. So what can you settle for? The grey shirt with the button-down collar? No. Though she liked it, it had that hand-me-down imprint in her mind, and since for some unknown reason, Melissa, despite being every bit as smart as her, hadn't won this award last year, she wasn't going to wear any of her hand-me-downs. That cut her choices to about half of her clothes. She picked out the navy blue skirt with the narrow white belt that fit through the loops at the waist and the white shirt she'd gotten from Shelby's brother when he'd outgrown it and Shelby hadn't wanted it because it was a boy's shirt — it buttoned on the wrong side and the sleeves required cufflinks.

Melissa returned while Leslie was putting the shirt on and said, "You shouldn't wear long sleeves in this hot weather, you'll swelter."

She wanted to say, "No, I won't. I'll be up on stage in the air-conditioned auditorium, gracefully receiving my award." Instead she said, "I'll roll them up, I always do."

Melissa didn't mention the award. One never knew in Leslie's family when people were having a lapse of memory, and while Melissa was reputed to have the best memory of them all, Leslie wouldn't have been surprised if she'd, almost deliberately, downright begrudgingly, forgotten this was the day for the award.

Fourth period, Leslie had been hit with a pop quiz in Civics — Mrs. Morrow's reminder that school wasn't out quite yet despite the way the midday heat bore down, making the earth smell strong of summer. As usual, she sat by the window. She bounced her foot with the jittery feeling she'd had all day waiting out the periods until sixth, when the assembly would occur. The heat was a drag but it calmed her; it slowed down the spinning of the panic wheels which turned inside her like the innards of a clock. She didn't see the student assistant coming, but suddenly there was someone beside her desk, a thin form of a girl. And when she looked up, she saw the neat paper with her name written on it. She felt as if she were having a lapse of memory herself. Hadn't this just happened to her the day before?

This time she *was* supposed to get up and follow. It took her a moment to work her legs. All the wheels inside speeded up and she didn't feel the floor beneath her feet as she followed her out. She worried should she tell Mrs. Morrow she hadn't finished her quiz, but the girl, whose name was Grace, signaled her with her finger, and the signal made her feel she was Grace's possession. She didn't know her. She knew she was an eighth grader. She knew this time it must be something awful; it must be whatever she'd thought it would be last time.

At the end of the corridor where they turned up toward the principal's office, the full strength of the sun entered her eyes before she could reach up to shade them. This was the only thing that made her unsure her mother was standing in the outer office, her white uniform just so, so white, her white shoes (polished that very morning before Leslie had even been awake) shining out the same white purity. Grace opened the door and held it for Leslie and heard only Leslie's gasp and, "Mom, what are you doing here?" before going on through to the principal's office. Leslie had an impulse to continue after her, passing by the woman in white.

"I brought you something," her mother chirped, too loud and cheery for Leslie's comfort.

"Nothing's wrong?" Leslie asked.

Her mother shook her head and smiled. Leslie was confused. Mothers didn't just come to school and call their kids out of class for nothing. Why didn't her mother know that?

"I'm trying to get off early enough to come to your assembly but in case I'm not able to, I brought you something to show how proud I am of you." Leslie's mother took a shiny white box out of a shopping bag and set it on the formica shelf, meant to hold kids' books and papers. She lifted out a large corsage and held it up to Leslie, caressing the petals of the carnations as she embraced them with her eyes.

"Oh, it's pretty. Aren't they pretty flowers." Leslie took it and smelled the flowers and looked it over carefully. In the aftermath of her words she recognized the imitation of how her mother would receive a gift. Even her voice had changed to sound like her mother's. She changed it back then, saying, "Thank you. That was nice of you." She handed her mother the corsage. "Could you please take it home for me?"

"Well, I thought you would wear it. I didn't get it to put in the refrigerator."

"But Mom, *nobody* wears a corsage around here, except for prom and we already had that last week." Leslie had thought she was finished with that wound. She hadn't gone because she hadn't been asked. Once the night itself was over, she'd emerged to face the world, telling herself she'd never have to think of it again. Now her mother wanted her to wear a prom corsage — probably purchased on sale at the florist's — to assembly. She felt so steamy hot, as if she were going to break into an oozing sweat any minute.

"You don't have to do things or not do things because everyone else does. It's your special day, your day to stand out, and I want you to wear this so when you go up for your award, everyone will know, someone thinks you're special."

"They'll already know," Leslie whispered to keep from shouting. She shifted her weight to her right hip as she had in the mirror to look tough and convincing. "They'll know enough."

Her mother brought forth her full scale guilt voice to counteract Leslie's posture. She looked hurt but crusty with her unwillingness to show it. "You don't want them to know you have a mother who cares?"

Leslie'd been accused; she wasn't required to answer. She didn't really want them to know anything about her mother. She wanted a mother who would be in the assembly, quietly watching, sending her a silent vote of assurance that she could walk across the stage without tripping. She wanted a mother dressed in street clothes so she wouldn't stand out, making it look as if a hospital had appeared in their midst. She wanted a mother who would tell her in the privacy of home how proud she was. Not here where the Civics quiz sat half done on her desk and everyone would want to know why she'd been called out, and the corsage was stuck between them, growing gigantic and less and less real with the passage of time. The flowers looked phony. Blue ones, pink ones. Leslie was sickened by the sweet odor that hung in the close air. She hardly recognized she was capable of such irreverence, but she thought it was a truly ugly corsage. She stood so that her body blocked it from view of anyone walking by the office. She felt like a basketball guard, alert for a quick move.

But she was not quick enough. "Just let me see how it looks," her mother said, reaching forward to pin in onto the right side of Leslie's shirt, which had a pocket on the left. Leslie felt like the donkey in pin-the-tail-on-the-donkey. The corsage pulled the shirt down and hung heavy on her small, round breast.

"No," she said, removing it. She laid it gently down to rest in its box.

"You keep it and decide," her mother said. "Think about it between now and then, and maybe you'll have a change of heart."

"I can't, Mom. I don't have anywhere to put it. I can't carry it into class, and I don't have time to go to my locker — I'm in the middle of a quiz in Civics." Her face was turning red: so much heat and desperation. She didn't want it to show. "Please," she said, shoving the box toward her mother. "Take it. I'm sorry."

But her mother slid it back toward her. "You take it. You're such a smart girl, you'll find some place for it." Her mother picked up her bag to leave.

Leslie was amazed how the words sprung out of her just in time. "If you leave it here, I'll throw it in the trash." She didn't want to hurt her more but saw that she had. She saw, as well, how the crust of her mother's expression hardened. Why couldn't her mother see she wasn't giving her any way out? Her mind was racing around, searching for a way to make this not be happening the way it was, seeking a cubbyhole somewhere in which to place this creepy corsage. She weighed her willingness to do whatever might make her mother feel better. Could she stand to make a fool of herself? Could she wear it to assembly, but take it off when she had to go up and get the prize? But that wouldn't satisfy her mother anyway. She wanted her to parade in it. Could she lie and say she'd worn it, while throwing it away? How then could she explain why she wasn't bringing it home? What good was a lie anyway? Underneath a lie you could only be fooled if you were willing to pretend things were different than they were.

No, awful as she felt, she wouldn't lie. She shifted her weight from where the heat was burning through the sole of her right foot.

Her mother's voice was wavery, wilted. "I have to go. I've spent my entire lunch hour coming up here . . . for this." She flicked her hand through the air to dismiss Leslie, then jabbed, "Melissa would have worn it proudly."

Leslie felt slapped. She remembered shock splintering the air the day Shelby's mother had suddenly turned into a viper, her hand darting forward with the speed of a snake's tongue to strike Shelby's face. She had watched the handprint come up gradually on Shelby's sallow skin, while Shelby and her mother had stood, eyes locked, steaming.

She wished her mother would slap her. It would help release her to move. She would rather have a handprint than this great numbing blush which stiffened her even while it made her feel like putty. She was afraid to speak, afraid if she did her mother would have another strike. She picked up the box, which nearly flew away it was so light. She felt too light herself, as if she were disappearing. She handed it to her mother, who took it. Leslie was satisfied that it was out of her hands. Now she only needed to turn and walk away. Hold her face together. Keep that little girl out of it. Get back to Civics and finish her quiz. She was full of determination, yet she couldn't move. She couldn't peel herself apart from her mother. She noticed how her mother's shoulders were held too rigidly, as if she had a spring wound up at the center of her back, and how the waist of her uniform was belted so it showed her stomach was trim and held in.

They stood and sang "America the Beautiful" to open the assembly. Singing with the rest gave her the sense of a belonger and when she sang, "God shed his grace on thee," her throat lumped up with a sweet kind of pain. As they were being seated, she turned to scan the audience. She was sure her mother wouldn't be there; still she had a precious fantasy in which her mother would realize she had wronged Leslie and leave the hospital, regardless of her work, to show up and watch her get her award.

She ran the fantasy through and let it float off from her. Then slowly, methodically, and with the victorious satisfaction of defiance, she unrolled her shirt sleeves and fixed the cuffs neatly with the cufflinks. The shirt had brought on her mother's last stab, which had made the break that let Leslie walk away. "What's *this* you're wearing for a special occasion?" Her mother'd fingered the rolled up sleeve. "I don't even know where you got this."

"You don't need to. It's mine," Leslie had replied.

Her mother had drilled her, going for the final word as she was about to clear the door. "Shoulders back," she'd commanded and Leslie's body had stiffened obediently.

Mr. Harrison ran through a string of announcements, but

169

Leslie hadn't heard a word until her name. She had to sidestep an obstacle path of knees to make it to the aisle. She concentrated on how the stiff, bright cuffs looked against the dark blue of her skirt as she held her hands folded in front of her and carefully placed one foot ahead of the other. She could hardly tell it was her moving, but someone in her body was going forward. Five steps up. She went to the center of the stage where Mr. Harrison handed her a flat piece of paper with a large gold medal stamped onto it. She felt in awe of the child who received it. She took one quick look out on the vast sea of people and listened to the noise and realized they were clapping for her. Just for the second she could spare to wish it without tears, she wished her mother was there.

She held her shoulders just so, the way she held them in her football jersey, as she walked back across the stage and eased down the stairs and down the aisle. She felt as if there were a bird inside her, flying. The bird said: you thought you'd fall on your face and you were actually graceful. The bird said: I heard them clapping for you.

Back in her seat, resuming ordinary life, she stared at the paper. The girl beside her said, "Let's see," and Leslie handed it over. Then she wished she hadn't because that girl gave it to the next one, and it was moving down the row, and Leslie's hands, sitting on her lap, felt so empty. Her mother always accused her imagination of being overly active, and perhaps she was right, because the shiny white corsage box appeared there to take up the empty space.

She dreaded having to go home to the corsage, how it would be in the refrigerator, wilting away for days. The pink tissue paper sticking out the edges of the box would get soiled from the food passing by it, and periodically her mother would take the corsage itself out and pluck away the deadest petals to freshen it up. If Leslie had any luck, this ritual of worship wouldn't take place before her eyes. Who would finally throw it away? Probably Melissa. Melissa, for her own reasons, would get sick of it taking up space and remove it from where it sat like the rotting thing it was between Leslie and her mother and dump it. Leslie imagined how she would step on it to squish it down in the trash can and the weak seams of the box would split open, revealing to anyone who wanted to see that it was nothing but an old, dead corsage.

Remembering Berlin — 1979

CAROL ASCHER

Even now I'm not sure what my mother and I wanted from our trip to Berlin, or what that wanting made us each deny. Mother had not been back to her native city for over forty years: since that day in 1938 when she left by train, a protected 21-year-old, sent into the unknown by her parents, who had not yet found a way for themselves to get out. On my own, I had once visited Berlin for a few days, found her old house, and searched for other clues to her past. For years, I had carried with me the wonderful stories of her enchanted childhood as the loved youngest daughter of a large prosperous family, fairy tales that turned my sister's and my Kansas childhood dull. On the other side, despite my own quiet childhood in a simple time, I lived in constant dread of losing everything I loved in some unknown holocaust. I would walk among the rubble of a totally destroyed city, the lone survivor. For years I had waited for this disaster.

In 1969, Willy Brandt, then Mayor of Berlin, initiated a special reparations program (in German, *Wiedergutmachen* — literally, to make good again) for those Berliners who escaped, or were taken away from, their city during National Socialism. Returnees are given a week in a hotel, a special tour of the city, tickets to a cultural event, and a luncheon with a representative of the Berlin Information Service.

In 1979, Mother retired from working as a nursery school teacher in Southern California. Now a widow, she had been talking about returning to Berlin under Willy Brandt's program. I urged her to apply and promised to go with her. Yet despite our mutual excitement about the trip, Mother could not get herself to write the necessary letter. When she wrote at last, it was late July and we wanted to go in September. She got a prompt reply from the Office of the Mayor. *"Sehr geehrte Frau Bergman,"* it began. Obviously, she was eligible, and they wanted very much to extend her an invitation. However, the program had become extremely popular, and priority was being given to old people and to those who had been sent to a concentration camp or had had to live underground. Should she remain intent on coming immediately, she would receive a modified program consisting of all but the hotel.

I think Mother was actually relieved to be denied something. After all, receiving the full compliment of hospitality seemed to imply a reciprocal obligation to accept that everything *had* been made good again. What she said, though, was characteristic: she didn't like burdening the contemporary German taxpayers, many of whom were too young to have been responsible for what had happened. Instead, like any well-seasoned traveler, she made reservations for us at a pension just off the elegant shopping street, Kurfurstendamn, only a few blocks from the apartment house her father had once owned and where she had grown up. After a brief trip on her own to Vienna to see my father's old home for the first time, she would meet me in Berlin.

It was pouring outside on the Friday morning my plane landed at Tegel Airport. I had only a small duffel bag, so I rushed quickly through customs. As I entered the general waiting area, I saw Mother beaming at me. Her hair, which she had recently stopped dying, was a surprisingly lovely icy gray; and she wore a new camel-colored coat she had bought especially for Berlin's chilly autumn. How many times in my Kansas childhood had I been ashamed of her sturdy, plain European looks. Now I thought she looked wonderful. At home with herself. Alive and elated. In her hand she held an orange rose. "Welcome to Berlin!" she said, hugging me. "I'm so glad you've come to see me here."

Mother jabbered nonstop on the double-decker bus from the airport, her speech flowing in a happy jumble of English and German. This street looked somewhat the same, she didn't remember it quite. That building over there, that was how everything had once been. So much was destroyed, but how nicely it had been built! On and on. Even the ruin of the Kaiser Gedächtnisskirche, with its new mosaic memorial towers, seemed to give her joy as the bus rumbled past.

We got off on the corner of the Kurfurstendamn and the small cross street of our pension. Exhausted from the night's travel, I imagined falling asleep for a couple of hours between clean sheets. At the building with the little sign, we climbed the three flights of worn stairs and rang the bell on the great carved wooden door. An elderly woman greeted us with stiff, embarrassed, nervousness. The Frau Kätner would be back in a few minutes. We could wait.

As Mother and I settled into the floral overstuffed chairs that crowded the front hall, Mother reminisced about her own home. The entrance to her family's apartment had been so much like this: a carved door there; the room adjacent to the hall, which here held neatly laid breakfast tables for the pension guests, would have been her family's *Musikzimmer;* the next room the *Herrenzimmer,* and so on down the hall we could barely see.

Now Frau Kätner in a heavy black coat let herself into the pension, greeting us as if distracted by a million other chores.

"I'm the woman who has returned to see my city, and this is my eldest daughter," Mother began enthusiastically, rising to her feet. When Frau Kätner continued to be distracted, Mother caught herself and hurriedly reminded her of our reservation.

"Ach ja," said Frau Kätner. The week was terribly busy — an industrial exhibit. For some reason she had been uncertain about the exact dates Mother would come. No, she had no more rooms. She didn't even know where else in the neighborhood we might find a place to stay.

We asked to leave our bags while we went back outside into the driving rain to look for other lodgings. I was exhausted, and the ignored reservation left me angry, humiliated, and suspicious. "Nazi!" I said under my breath, as we climbed back down the long flight of sagging wooden stairs.

Mother gave me a sharp look — "You're not going to have a good time here if you have that attitude" — and took my arm.

For the next hour, we climbed up and down the wide, once elegant, inner wooden stairs of five- and six-story buildings. Each time the carved doors of a pension opened, Mother rang out her whole story: she had come back to Berlin after 40 years, I was her oldest daughter just arrived from New York, the reservation for four nights which she had made so carefully at another pension had not been kept. The hidden pain of her repeated saga made me jittery and nervous; why expose ourselves to people who, at best, clicked their tongues sympathetically at our homeless state?

Finally, just as we were about to take a bus out of the neighborhood to a central lodging bureau, a middle-aged woman in a patriotic red and green Tyrol jumper opened her heavy wooden door. Pleasantly, but briskly, she said yes.

(Had we heard right?) Yes, she did have a free room for the length of our stay. Mother smiled at me in triumph, and my shoulders relaxed. While she signed the registration, I collapsed on the bed. Then we went back out into the rain to collect our bags.

Like my sisters, I had been worried about Mother's return. Still, I remember Miriam, my youngest sister, joking over the telephone that Mother would probably discover the good in Berlin and ward off the sad or bad. When we were children, Mother used to laugh at herself for being a Pollyanna. Although cousins, aunts, and uncles had all perished in Auschwitz, even the War had turned out well for her — as she said, for she had fallen in love with our father in an English internment camp, and they had been happy until he died. Something in her childhood had given her the gift or the plague to see the sunny side of things. Why then did her oldest daughter yearn to understand the dark?

In the afternoon, after a hot meal in a beer hall, we turned off the Kurfurstendamn onto a side street where Mother's family's synagogue had stood. I would have passed it, if Mother had not touched my arm. On our right stood a low concrete building that looked more like a social service center or a public school. Only after a moment did I notice a broken stone arch over its front doorway and a lone chipped stone pillar standing off to the side on the lawn.

"That's all that's left," Mother said matter-of-factly.

Then her voice grew warm: her four brothers had been bar mitzvahed in the synagogue. Also every High Holy Day the whole family — aunts, uncles, everyone — had walked there together from their home. At Sukkoth, the back of the synagogue had been turned into a beautiful arbor from which apples and pears were hung. Under the sukkoth, one ate delicious challah and looked up and saw the stars!

"Want to go in?" I asked, wanting to pull together her

happy reminiscence and the scene before us.

"Not right now," she said.

It is nearly eleven o'clock on our first night in Berlin, and we have returned tired but exhilarated from a violin concert at the newly built Philharmonic Hall. Mother takes off her knit suit, laying it carefully over the chair. I look over at her in her bra and panties as I pull off my own sweater and slacks. I am surprised by her youthful body. Although she is not slim, her flesh has remained round and buoyant. I feel pleased, more secure about how my own body will look in thirty years. Mother has been looking at me too. Neither of us has seen each other without clothes in years. "You are thin," she says. "Last year when you were in California, you were plump, and it was nice. You work too hard." It is true that I have been working hard, taking on extra work. But I actually like my body leaner.

We crawl under our thick goose down comforters. I try to draw into myself, but Mother is alive with memories. The high ceiling of our yellow pension room reminds her of the pulleys with which all seven children's bicycles were hung from her family's ceiling. The courtyard below our window has the same neat paths and flower patches as hers did. There was a pet parrot — I have never heard of him. One Pessach the parrot died from eating matsah, and she herself buried him in the courtyard garden.

I fall asleep.

We were sitting silently in our wooden coats and jackets in the Berlin Information Service minibus, squeezed in with six other Jews from Los Angeles, New York, and Haifa, who would also see their home town on this chilly fall day. West Berlin, even sliced off from its eastern half, is still vast and sprawling. A back packer who had taken Berlin by foot on my first visit, I had seen only little clumps here and there and had no clear idea of how the city fans out into working-class districts, elegant suburbs, parklands, lakes and waterways. Nor had I visited the various civic and war memorials at which our minibus now stopped.

The Plotzensee Memorial Museum lies just outside the red brick walls of the Plotzensee penitentiary, which is largely hidden from view by a new road system which diverts traffic in a series of under- and over-passes. Getting out of the minibus, we entered a kind of large brick garage in which several thousand people had been guillotined or hung during the Third Reich — the guillotine and hooks are still there — and where German military leaders hid in the last months of the War while plotting (unsuccessfully) to overthrow Hitler. On some walls, displays recount the histories of those who were brought to death in the building. Since my reading in German is slow, Mother helped me with some of the stories. Then we walked behind the building to a terrace which holds an urn of ashes taken from the death camps, and a twelve-foot-high oblong granite memorial, "to the millions of sacrifices of the Third Reich, who because of their political convictions, their religious beliefs, or their heritage, were defamed, mishandled, robbed of their freedom, or murdered."

"They don't go out of their way to mention Jews," I said to Mother, feeling bewildered and resentful at how both inside and outside Jews seemed to have become hidden from the history.

"That's what makes it so impressive," Mother answered, deep in reassuring thought. "The German people today recognize that it was everybody."

The others were already back in their seats in the minibus when Mother and I joined them. As we drove off onto a higher road, we gained our first full view of Plotzensee Prison, which, as our guide had explained, was now filled with German teenagers.

In the late morning the rain had begun to come down

heavily, and the windshield wipers cut rhythmically into our guide's talk. At the edge of vacant lots, huge warehouses, and printing plants, we came to a stop beside several large tour buses. A small low building seemed to hold a luncheonette, and postcards were laid out on a stand under its eaves. As we tumbled out of the minibus, I noticed people with opened umbrellas winding their way up a narrow stairs which led to an overlook at the top of a twelve-foot-high wall that divides East Berlin from West Berlin.

Arriving at the top, I looked out over a muddy waste. Perhaps fifty yards away a line of electrified barbed wire followed the Wall, and another fifty yards beyond that there was still another barbed wire fence. Finally, at yet another similar distance, a second wall made the final separation between the East and the West. Several men in military coats walked along the mud. Beyond the second wall, I could see the vast gray stone public buildings, once part of my mother's Berlin, and the new high-rises of socialist housing.

But now as we crept gingerly back down the stairs, cautioning each other not to slip, I heard the man from California showing his son a large graffiti on the wall by the steps.

NSDAP 卐 FREIHEIT

ran the sign. The son nodded quietly. I pointed out the sign to Mother. "I saw it," she said tensely.

Half an hour later we were driving through a district of modest four-story houses and commercial buildings.

"My father's factory was down that street." Mother quietly pointed out the window.

My grandfather's vacuum sweeper plant had been slowly stripped from him in the years after 1933. Finally in 1940, a year after *Kristallnacht,* my grandfather and grandmother had escaped with a few Persian rugs and their *milschig* and *fleischig* silverware in a closed train that traveled through

Russia and China; at Shanghai, they caught a boat to Mexico, where my grandfather died of malaria. My newly widowed grandmother was living with us in Kansas when we heard that the vacuum sweeper factory had been bombed.

"Tell him to drive by the building," I urged.

The guide was lecturing, and Mother was reluctant to interrupt.

"Mother!" I said.

When the man paused, Mother began, "I wonder if you would be so kind. My father's factory was at 37 Waldstrasse. The building no longer stands. But my daughter would like to see where it once stood."

The driver turned onto a quiet block with a strip of grass down the middle of the street, lined by pinkish buildings. The minibus was driving slowly so that everyone could read the small numbers on the buildings. "Thirty-one," "Thirty-three," "Thirty-five," our car mates whispered as we inched our way down the street.

"Thirty-five is still standing," said Mother, pointing out the old decorative molding on the pale pink concrete.

"Thirty-nine looks like the original," said someone in the van.

"Yes, but it's thirty-seven," said Mother. No one had even noticed the plain new building faded between the other numbers.

I thought Mother might want to get out of the car, or at least would say something to all of us about her last years on the street. No one in the minibus understood that she had also lived there, behind the machines. Someone asked what they had manufactured in the factory. Then the driver sped on.

But my thoughts lingered around the building on Waldstrasse. Why had Mother been so shy about directing us to it, and so quiet, almost disinterested, once we were there? I knew only the outlines of how she had come to live at Waldstrasse. As her older siblings had left home to study in countries where the universities still allowed Jews, my grandfather had thought to move to a smaller house. Finding an apartment on Kaiserdamn, the remaining family had moved in. But soon they had noticed the black limousines come and go on the street and discovered that Göring lived beneath them. Meanwhile, my grandfather had sold the apartment building in Wilmersdorf, and, because he was also having trouble with his factory, he began to carve out a little apartment in the back. It was here that my mother had spent her last six years in Germany, finding little handicrafts to occupy her time because she herself was no longer allowed to attend school. It was here on Waldstrasse that the Nazis had forcibly collected my grandfather's vacuum sweeper parts as "junk" for the Third Reich, and here that my grandfather had been pulled out of his bed night after night to be ridiculed and then tortured at Gestapo Headquarters. Other things must have happened on Waldstrasse that I knew nothing about. I hardly knew how I had gotten her to tell me this.

In the afternoon, Mother and I returned to Charlottenberg, where we strolled through the Palace museums. "I remember this! I saw it with Papa. But it wasn't here," Mother would exclaim, and then recall with amazing certainty how the object or picture had been in another Berlin museum before the bombings. When I was a child, Mother had allowed her poor memory to become an object for family sport. Yet now I saw how excellent it might have been, not torn from its web of association.

When we tired of the museums, we roamed between the peddlers' stalls in the flea market across from the Palace. Here were piles of heavy old velvet curtains, tarnished but elaborate silverware, soup tureens, candelabra, old fur coats, ancient yellowing underwear trimmed with handmade lace, woolen sweaters, and brightly colored crystal goblets.

"Tsk! We had those in my house." Mother kept pointing

with awe and disgust.

She had discovered a tiny silver egg cup just like she had
had at home and wanted to take it back to Miriam. But she
could not get herself to buy it. "It's not nice to buy a gift in a
flea market," she finally said, as if our family adhered to some
refined standard of gift giving; yet a moment later I realized
the resentment even she didn't perceive, of symbolically
buying back a family item.

On Sunday, our third day, it was still cold and wet.
Climbing out of the subway into a genteel residential area
called Dahlem, we walked a few blocks through soaked red
leaves to the Staatliche Museum. There we spent three or four
hours focusing on one painting after another with a concentration and harmony that neither of us, in our often stormy and
irritated relationship, had ever experienced together.

When we came out of the museum, the weather had
cleared and we decided to walk awhile. The streets of Dahlem
are broad and tree-lined. Dense ivy, which glows a brilliant
red in fall, covers the gracious large houses surrounded by
small gardens and elegant wrought-iron fences. Although the
names on the gates indicate that many have been converted
into multiple dwellings, there is still an air of luxury and ease.
Mother talked about her childhood friends who had lived in
Dahlem. "Would some of your Christian school friends still
live here?" "Yes," she thought so. "Do you want to try to visit
one?" "No." She knew the neighborhood so well that she
began to test herself playfully by predicting the names of the
streets.

At Roseneck, we looked for a *Konditerei,* where her father had taken the seven children for a treat on Sunday
mornings. Like detectives, we paced back and forth along the
brick corner building where Mother was certain the cake shop
had once been. Now the building held a bank. Finally, a gleam
of success in her eyes, Mother showed me how the windows

were table height! They would surely never have been built just like this for a bank.

As we turned down the street, Mother abruptly said, "If you notice any of my reactions, you should tell them to me."

I didn't understand what she meant, and then I realized she was asking me to put into words the fleeting emotions she was unable to trap or express. My heart went out to her, at the same time as I felt on guard. I had struggled so hard, was still struggling, to be separate from her, and now she wanted me to give up my point of view and live inside her skin.

"You don't give me much to go on," I said, noncommittally.

"Yes, but maybe sometimes an expression crosses my eyes —?"

"Most of the time," I said, knowing I was about to fail her, but unable to give up my hard-won separateness. "Most of the time, when you don't have a happy memory, you seem to keep quiet."

Mother and I have a conversation over and over. We see a woman, man, or couple her age, and she sighs, "Na, I wonder what they suffered during the War."

"Maybe they were Nazis," I casually reply, struck by how well-dressed these Berliners are, eating cake with whipped cream in their expensive cafes.

"Carol, you can't know what they did. And the War—the rations, the bombing — was terrible for everyone. I was actually lucky not to live through any of it."

"I think you're projecting, because you're unable to face your own suffering," I say to her.

But she insists that she didn't suffer as much as those who lived in Berlin during the War years.

And, on my side, walking arm-in-arm along Berlin's streets, I am compelled to lecture her on the history of anti-Semitism in Germany, Austria, and Poland. Dutifully nodding, Mother sometimes says, "I admire your capacity to read and remember so much. I never could do that." But if I continue too long, she shakes her head. "I don't see what drives you to learn all this."

On Sunday evening, we walked to the Berlin Opera House to see Beethoven's *Fidelio*. This was our third night of music, and we were paying for our own tickets now, but Mother seemed hungry for any culture we could take in.

Fidelio is set in 18th century Spain in a fortress for the confinement of political prisoners. Leonora, disguised as a man (Fidelio), becomes a warden in order to find her husband, who is being starved in the prison's dungeon. The stage throughout is dark and gloomy; one is never out of the shadow of those fortress walls. To break the relentless gloom, a (to me irritating) subplot revolves around the prison warden's daughter's infatuation with Fidelio. Yet there are few musical moments as glorious as the last chorus: Fidelio, her husband, the prisoners, even the prison officials, all singing to the triumph of justice and a woman's courage.

Tears streamed helplessly down my face as I thought of all the walls we'd seen over the last days.

"Think of how terrible to find you've been so fooled." Mother broke into my watery grandeur of feeling.

When I understood her meaning, I was shocked. Mother had been identifying with the naiveté of the prison warden's daughter. For her, the opera had been about how the desire to love can lead to a totally false evaluation of the object of that love.

Monday we were to lunch with a representative of the Information Service — it would be, I realized, our first long talk with someone besides each other since we had come to Berlin. Mother was very nervous. She thought we should prepare questions. And she was worried about my behavior until I promised not to raise topics that would embarrass the man. We arrived at the elegant Berlin Hotel half an hour early and went into the lounge of the women's bathroom, where I helped her write down things to ask, mostly about the War years when she was no longer there. (It seemed that she could reminisce about her charming childhood, or wonder about her troubled city after she had left, but she could barely touch on that dark period from 1933 to 1938 when she was becoming a young woman alone at the back of a factory.)

At exactly one-thirty, we came out of the bathroom, washed and combed and conscious of wearing our best traveling clothes. Crossing the heavily carpeted lobby, we saw a slim gray-haired man in a well-tailored beige suit sitting at one of the tables near the restaurant door, an elegant leather briefcase on his lap.

"I bet that's him," Mother whispered.

The man looked like an art dealer to me.

Suddenly, as if scenting something of 'the returned refugee' about us, the *maitre d'* rushed towards us, and in a moment he was introducing us to the gray-haired man, who had stood in greeting.

"Grüss Gott, küss die Hand," he said, holding Mother's hand to his lips. *"Sehr geehrte gnädiga Frau Bergman. Ich bin entzückt Ihnen kennen zu lehrnen."*

Never since my Austrian grandmother was alive had I heard such a profusion of pleasantries! Even I was included: *"die reizende Tochter, die so freundlich ist, ihrer Mutter nach Berlin zu begleiten."*

Herr Dietz went on smiling and chatting as we settled in our velvet chairs under the heavy crystal chandeliers. We folded our linen napkins on our laps. Then he advised us on what was tastiest on the menu. "Order first and talk later," he smiled, showing his perfect teeth. Mother followed his suggestion of a veal in sauce, but I gave vent to petty rebellion and ordered something else.

When the menus had been taken away, Herr Dietz folded his well-kept hands over his platter and gave us a long smile of satisfaction. "And so, Frau Bergman, how do you find Berlin?"

Mother glowed: Berlin had changed in many ways; she gave examples. It was still so much the way she remembered it; she gave other examples. He asked her about places she would surely have known — the Olympic stadium, the *Tiergarten* — and she told him whether or not we had been able to see them on this trip. Soon they were verbally scrambling over the city together, he offering a memory and an observation, she another memory, another question. Mother was becoming increasingly animated and lively, almost girlish. Was it partly, I wondered, the attention of a man her own age, now so rare in her widowed life? Or was she letting herself imagine, for one brief luncheon, that she might have lived here, had a right to, her beloved city?

As waiters in black tuxedos brought our meals on silver platters, Herr Dietz answered Mother's lively questions with long personal stories about his own life. He was from Silesia, which now lay in East Germany. He had served in the army in the early '40s and had married a school teacher. His daughter was married to a Jew. The War had been hard: he and his wife had had to search for food for their children. One entire night of bombings he had spent in a basement with his niece in his arms. Nothing in his life, even serving at the front, had been worse than the bombs. "You were in World War I?" asked Mother, unable to take in that her luncheon mate had been so nearly her enemy. "No, World War II," he said, for the second time. Then he talked about the months after the War when Berliners realized that their city would be divided. There was constant travel back and forth as people tried to settle hurriedly in the sector where they felt safest. In a largely destroyed city, where housing was already tight, living became horribly crowded. Then one day in 1961 the Wall began to go up, much of it constructed with the remaining rubble of bombed buildings.

To prolong our luncheon, Mother and I had ordered rich desserts of heavy whipped cream, which we spooned idly while Herr Dietz sipped his black saccharined coffee. Then as the unfinished cream melted in our cut glass dishes, Mother and Herr Dietz talked on and on. Yet it was odd how neither had touched on the experience of Jews in Berlin or why, specifically, Mother had suddenly left her city and aging parents. Was it the tact of *Wiedergutmachen* to speak to only those subjects the returnee introduced? Now it was after 3:30, and I sensed that it was time for Herr Dietz to return to his office, but that he could not be the one to end the luncheon. Finally, I broke in with my best German:

"You've been good to give us your time. I'm sure you have other obligations."

That seemed sufficient to end the luncheon. Five minutes later, after a number of Grüsses, we had said goodbye to Herr Dietz and were putting on our coats.

Mother was in a jubilant mood. As we struck out across the grassy plaza in front of the Berlin Hotel, she kept saying, "Carol, that was just great! Just great! You didn't think it was wonderful?" she said at last, catching my hesitation.

"Not really," I admitted. "Though I'm not sure what else it could have been."

A memory lingers of a place I did not go with Mother. I play the moment of decision over and over, trying to alter the outcome. We are walking toward the subway station, a block away from Mother's childhood home in Wilmersdorf. "Shall we just go by and see it?" she asks, telling me in the same breath that she saw it that morning before I arrived. "No, it's not necessary. I saw it too when I was here before," I reply, imagining the five-story stucco building with its luxurious, strangely modern windows. And we walk on to the subway, never having stood together on the wooded middle-class street and looked up at the windows of the rooms in which she grew up.

If I Lived
in Maine

PEGGY SHINNER

I don't remember what I remember anymore. I remember that she said stress causes cancer. Stress causes cancer she said. I remember that she said her children were a source of stress. Did she say that? Did she really say that? Perhaps I said that. Perhaps I insinuated. I led her on. You have a lot of stress in your life. Your children cause you stress. And she said yes, that's right. My children cause me stress. By your children you mean me. Is that what you mean? I cause you stress. You cause me stress she said. Stress causes cancer. I remember that she said I cause her stress because I'm a lesbian. You're a lesbian. That causes stress. Stress causes cancer. That's what she said. At the very least suggested. She implied it. Even if she couldn't say it. She hinted. I said it. She had stress. Yes. She got cancer. Yes. I'm a lesbian.

She read in the newspaper that stress causes cancer. That it lowers your immunities. Certain people are prone to stress.

Prone to cancer. She told me she read it in a newspaper. Maybe she didn't remember correctly. Maybe I don't remember. Maybe I dreamed it. I heard it in a dream. In the dream she accuses me. She blames me for who I am and then tells me it's through no fault of her own. She blames me for choosing. When I wake up from the dream she is smiling. She says we are alike. She says she just wants me to be happy. That's what every mother wants. I remember she said that. For me she wanted only happiness. For her I wanted three more months.

She read it in the newspaper. I heard it on the radio. Stress causes cancer. A man's parents got divorced and he got malignant melanoma. For his cure, he took up comedy. He's a comedian. Now he tells his story on public radio stations. He stars in clubs. He starts his act by showing the audience the spot on his back where the melanoma began. Fifty percent of marriages end in divorce he says, lifting his shirt, and revealing his white, liver-spotted flesh.

I remember her silence. I remember how she drove in silence and then she said I'll never forget this as long as I live. She kept driving. She drove thirty in a thirty-five-mile-per-hour zone. A boy once told me that how you drive is how you have sex. He said I was frigid when I didn't want to kiss him. He said if you can't whistle you're frigid. He leaned over at every stoplight and pushed his tongue in my mouth. His middle finger was cut off at the knuckle. I imagined the tip of it turning in the lawn mower blades. He couldn't do fuck you with that hand. Sitting on the tennis court, he moved his chopped-off hand toward me on the ground. His finger tried to probe my ass. He counted one, two, three. In bed at night I tried to whistle but no sound came out. I wanted to ask her if I was frigid but I couldn't. I asked her what's 69. I asked her what's a climax. I asked her to show me a rubber and she filled it up with water. She told me that sex was an expression of love and that men liked it better. She told me to keep my legs crossed.

She drove in silence. She made no left turns and would not drive on the expressway. She only drove on streets she had driven on before. When the light was green she slowed down in case it turned red. Her license plates were her initials and her address.

She said I'll never forget this as long as I live. I thought once what it would be like if she died. It would be like if I lived in Maine. We would be states apart; I would never talk to her but she would be there. I could visit whenever I wanted. If I lived in Maine, her silence couldn't be used against me. She would never snub me. If I lived in Maine for as long as I lived, she would miss me. She would invite me home and never accuse me of leaving too early. She would look forward to my visits and tell everyone I was coming. Her daughter who lived in Maine. If I lived in Maine I could move back whenever I wanted.

At the corner of Lincoln and Touhy. Her hands high on the steering wheel. Staring straight ahead. What? I said. What are you talking about? Purple hands with long, slender fingers, veins like rivers. Silence. Cars passing on the left. We hugged the right hand land. Answer me. What do you mean? On our way to Loehmann's. She wanted to buy me a sweater. She said I needed clothes. We stopped at three-way intersections; we waited for the lights to change. You just can't say something like that and think you can get away with it. We pulled into the parking lot. She sat with the key in the ignition. I'll never forget this as long as I live. Suddenly she turned to me. Her face looked pale even with make-up. If you don't know, she said, I can't tell you.

My mother said never sleep with a cat because it could suffocate you in the middle of the night. Sleep with me she said. But I wasn't tired when I slept with her. I never slept. I lay awake in the middle of her bed, with her breath blowing in my face. My head was turned to the left. In my bed I always slept on the right. That's how I remember it. But maybe that was after. I was ten then. What could I tell her? I'm not tired? I'm not sleepy? I wanted to be sleepy. I wanted to fall asleep. I wanted to get up. Sometimes she flung her arm across my waist. She had long, heavy arms. When she held them up, they swung back and forth underneath. She hated her arms. She had electrolysis once on her forearms. It left her with oddly spaced long, black hairs. She said she saw stars.

She wanted me to face her. She wanted us to take naps together like mothers and daughters do she said. She said I was a cold fish. She said I wasn't natural. I lay awake with my eyes closed. With my eyes open. Her breath came in spurts from her nose. It covered my face like a towel. I wanted to turn away. If I turned away, I could look into her closet and count the pairs of shoes. I could see her dresses and remember when she'd worn them. I used to watch her get dressed for going out to dinner on Saturday night. She would wear black or navy or brown and pick out her hair with a bobby pin. She pursed her lips together to spread the lipstick evenly. She had a charm bracelet with the 14 kt. gold heads of a girl and a boy. Our names and birthdays were engraved on the back.

It was the middle of the afternoon and light came through the window. If I listened I could hear a car. I wonder now if she was tired.

Three things I remember more than anything. I remember the night before Benny was born, when I slept in the kitchen on the hide-a-bed. I leaned my head against the refrigerator door, the bed was flush against it. I was wearing my airplane pajamas and the big straw hat. The bed took up the whole room.

The next day they brought Benny home from the hospital. They could hardly squeeze in the kitchen. He had a fat bald head and blue eyes. I'd never seen blue eyes before. Everyone always said he looked adopted.

I was playing in the front of the house. "A" my name is. A ten-speed bike ran over me. It seemed to take a long time. From foot to head. I kept my eyes closed. I remember its thin wheels on my body. I felt flattened, pressed. My arms were splayed out to the sides. I don't remember a rider or any sound. Afterwards, I got up and played.

When I had my tonsils out, they rolled me down basement corridors lined with shelves of gray cloth bags soaked through with blood. That's where they kept all the tonsils. I was looking for mine.

Near the end of radiation I bought her an umbrella. It was oversized, like a beach umbrella, with green and white alternating wedges. It wasn't her color but all the dark ones were collapsible and cheap. In her closet there was a raincoat with the price tag and extra button hanging from it; she'd bought it on a day she managed to lug herself to Loehmann's. That night I made her scrambled eggs for supper because they were easy to eat she said. I put the soft cooked eggs in the blender.

She was sunk against the arm of the couch when I gave her the package. Her face and hair looked sticky yellow; her slippered feet were tucked under her loose-as-jelly thighs. Every morning she labored from the bedroom to the bathroom and then spent the day propped on the couch in the den. She swallowed and whispered. Sometimes she wrote notes.

I encouraged her to tear off the wrapping but she merely swatted at it. When I asked her if she needed help, she said why don't you. I told her try to do it yourself. She closed her eyes and seemed to fall asleep for a second. I used to sleep in this room but now I didn't live here. The room had been my bedroom, with matching bedspread and laminated window shades. Once I had a peeping tom. A boy with red scars on his face tried to cut the screen. I wondered how long he'd been standing there with his face pressed against the window and what he'd seen me do. I tried to recount my actions but I couldn't remember. I felt afraid and flattered. People were always telling me what a good figure I had. When I was ten, a neighbor had commented on it. I said thank you.

Finally she opened her eyes. The partially exposed umbrella lay foolishly across her lap. I was perched against the desk waiting for her to be pleased.

In the hospital I took elevators up and down to floors she wasn't on. I watched people get in and out, pinched faces, clutching flowers or a box of Fanny May. It was like driving a long distance but I covered the same ground. The swish of doors. Opening. Closing. Semper discretus. All of us mute, averting. Then the flap of a hospital gown, shuffle of slippers with feet following behind. Once the doors wouldn't open. The elevator went up and down without stopping. I pressed all the buttons, any floor, it didn't matter. I pressed emergency. A voice filled the elevator; it came from nowhere. Don't panic. Be calm. We hit bottom and the doors opened into a tunnel hallway of ducts and dim light. I pressed my mother's floor.

As a child I would never take an escalator going down. I was afraid of putting one foot on the top step and being split in two. My mother pulled me by the hand as we hurried down aisles looking for elevators.

She said of Benny, talking to Benny was almost like having a daughter. She said that to me. I remember. She said I was like no daughter no mother ever had. Why can't you be the same? She said Carol, her co-worker, was like a daughter to her. She said Holly, her best friend's daughter, was the best daughter a mother could have. She said you won't let me be your mother. She said please.

I have no memory of her. When I close my eyes I get no picture. She's never in my dreams. If she is, she's dying. When I wake up, the dream is gone. There's only one thing I remember. I don't really know if I remember it. Maybe it's just a wish. A desire. Maybe it's not memory at all. How can I tell the difference between what happened and something I just remember? How can I verify? She was in the hospital. We were alone. She asked me for her make-up case. Her shiny floral make-up bag. On Saturday nights, I heard the clicking sound of the plastic cases. Lipstick against mascara. Tortoise shell blush-on case. They clicked like pleasant tongues. When she was out, I rummaged through the mysteries. Eye shadow and liner. Tubes and boxes and round, prim cases. Plastic clacking. Satisfaction. Now we were in the hospital. I wanted to go home. When I was home, I wanted to go back. I pushed myself out of the vinyl chair. She pointed to the closet with drawers. Bring it to me she said. She held the air. I gave her the make-up bag. She fumbled through its contents. Lipstick pressed in her fingers. Clotted breathing. Hold the mirror. She started at the corner of her mouth and moved toward the middle. She rolled her lips together. The lipstick was red and her fingers drained. When she finished she looked smaller. Gashed. She smiled at me. I thought it was a smile. A slight, sad upturning. She didn't ask me to kiss her but I would have. I would have forced myself.

The White Umbrella

GISH JEN

When I was twelve, my mother went to work without telling me or my little sister.

"Not that we need the second income." The lilt of her accent drifted from the kitchen up to the top of the stairs, where Mona and I were listening.

"No," said my father, in a barely audible voice. "Not like the Lee family."

The Lees were the only other Chinese family in town. I remembered how sorry my parents had felt for Mrs. Lee when she started waitressing downtown the year before; and so when my mother began coming home late, I didn't say anything, and tried to keep Mona from saying anything either.

"But why shouldn't I?" she argued. "Lots of people's mothers work."

"Those are American people," I said.

"So what do you think we are? I can do the pledge of

allegiance with my eyes closed."

Nevertheless, she tried to be discreet; and if my mother wasn't home by 5:30, we would start cooking by ourselves, to make sure dinner would be on time. Mona would wash the vegetables and put on the rice; I would chop.

For weeks we wondered what kind of work she was doing. I imagined that she was selling perfume, testing dessert recipes for the local newspaper. Or maybe she was working for the florist. Now that she had learned to drive, she might be delivering boxes of roses to people.

"I don't think so," said Mona as we walked to our piano lesson after school. "She would've hit something by now."

A gust of wind littered the street with leaves.

"Maybe we better hurry up," she went on, looking at the sky. "It's going to pour."

"But we're too early." Her lesson didn't begin until 4:00, mine until 4:30, so we usually tried to walk as slowly as we could. "And anyway, those aren't the kind of clouds that rain. Those are cumulus clouds."

We arrived out of breath and wet.

"Oh, you poor, poor dears," said old Miss Crosman. "Why don't you call me the next time it's like this out? If your mother won't drive you, I can come pick you up."

"No, that's okay," I answered. Mona wrung her hair out on Miss Crosman's rug. "We just couldn't get the roof of our car to close, is all. We took it to the beach last summer and got sand in the mechanism." I pronounced this last word carefully, as if the credibility of my lie depended on its middle syllable. "It's never been the same." I thought for a second. "It's a convertible."

"Well then make yourselves at home." She exchanged looks with Eugenie Roberts, whose lesson we were interrupting. Eugenie smiled good-naturedly. "The towels are in the closet across from the bathroom."

Huddling at the end of Miss Crosman's nine-foot

leatherette couch, Mona and I watched Eugenie play. She was a grade ahead of me and, according to school rumor, had a boyfriend in high school. I believed it. Aside from her ballooning breasts — which threatened to collide with the keyboard as she played — she had auburn hair, blue eyes, and, I noted with a particular pang, a pure white folding umbrella.

"I can't see," whispered Mona.

"So clean your glasses."

"My glasses *are* clean. You're in the way."

I looked at her. "They look dirty to me."

"That's because *your* glasses are dirty."

Eugenia came bouncing to the end of her piece.

"Oh! Just stupendous!" Miss Crosman hugged her, then looked up as Eugenie's mother walked in. "Stupendous!" she said again. "Oh! Mrs. Roberts! Your daughter has a gift, a real gift. It's an honor to teach her."

Mrs. Roberts, radiant with pride, swept her daughter out of the room as if she were royalty, born to the piano bench. Watching the way Eugenie carried herself, I sat up, and concentrated so hard on sucking in my stomach that I did not realize until the Robertses were gone that Eugenie had left her umbrella. As Mona began to play, I jumped up and ran to the window, meaning to call to them — only to see their brake lights flash then fade at the stop sign at the corner. As if to allow them passage, the rain had let up; a quivering sun lit their way.

The umbrella glowed like a scepter on the blue carpet while Mona, slumping over the keyboard, managed to eke out a fair rendition of a catfight. At the end of the piece, Miss Crosman asked her to stand up.

"Stay right there," she said, then came back a minute later with a towel to cover the bench. "You must be cold," she continued. "Shall I call your mother and have her bring over some dry clothes?"

"No," answered Mona. "She won't come because she . . ."

"She's too busy," I broke in from the back of the room.

"I see." Miss Crosman sighed and shook her head a little. "Your glasses are filthy, honey," she said to Mona. "Shall I clean them for you?"

Sisterly embarrassment seized me. Why hadn't Mona wiped her lenses when I told her to? As she resumed abuse of the piano, I stared at the umbrella. I wanted to open it, twirl it around by its slender silver handle; I wanted to dangle it from my wrist on the way to school the way the other girls did. I wondered what Miss Crosman would say if I offered to bring it to Eugenie at school tomorrow. She would be impressed with my consideration for others; Eugenie would be pleased to have it back; and I would have possession of the umbrella for an entire night. I looked at it again, toying with the idea of asking for one for Christmas. I knew, however, how my mother would react.

"Things," she would say. "What's the matter with a raincoat? All you want is things, just like an American."

Sitting down for my lesson, I was careful to keep the towel under me and sit up straight.

"I'll bet you can't see a thing either," said Miss Crosman, reaching for my glasses. "And you can relax, you poor dear." She touched my chest, in an area where she never would have touched Eugenie Roberts. "This isn't a boot camp."

When Miss Crosman finally allowed me to start playing I played extra well, as well as I possibly could. See, I told her with my fingers. You don't have to feel sorry for me.

"That was wonderful," said Miss Crosman. "Oh! Just wonderful."

An entire constellation rose in my heart.

"And guess what," I announced proudly. "I have a surprise for you."

Then I played a second piece for her, a much more

difficult one that she had not assigned.

"Oh! That was stupendous," she said without hugging me. "Stupendous! You are a genius, young lady. If your mother had started you younger, you'd be playing like Eugenie Roberts by now!"

I looked at the keyboard, wishing that I had still a third, even more difficult piece to play for her. I wanted to tell her that I was the school spelling bee champion, that I wasn't ticklish, that I could do karate.

"My mother is a concert pianist," I said.

She looked at me for a long moment, then finally, without saying anything, hugged me. I didn't say anything about bringing the umbrella to Eugenie at school.

The steps were dry when Mona and I sat down to wait for my mother.

"Do you want to wait inside?" Miss Crosman looked anxiously at the sky.

"No," I said. "Our mother will be here any minute."

"In a while," said Mona.

"Any minute," I said again, even though my mother had been at least twenty minutes late every week since she started working.

According to the church clock across the street we had been waiting twenty-five minutes when Miss Crosman came out again.

"Shall I give you ladies a ride home?"

"No," I said. "Our mother is coming any minute."

"Shall I at least give her a call and remind her you're here? Maybe she forgot about you."

"I don't think she *forgot*," said Mona.

"Shall I give her a call anyway? Just to be safe?"

"I bet she already left," I said. "How could she forget about us?"

Miss Crosman went in to call.

"There's no answer," she said, coming back out.

"See, she's on her way," I said.

"Are you sure you wouldn't like to come in?"

"No," said Mona.

"Yes," I said. I pointed at my sister. "She meant yes too. She meant no, she wouldn't like to go in."

Miss Crosman looked at her watch. "It's 5:30 now, ladies. My pot roast will be coming out in fifteen minutes. Maybe you'd like to come in and have some then?"

"My mother's almost here," I said. "She's on her way."

We watched and watched the street. I tried to imagine what my mother was doing; I tried to imagine her writing messages in the sky, even though I knew she was afraid of planes. I watched as the branches of Miss Crosman's big willow tree started to sway; they had all been trimmed to exactly the same height off the ground, so that they looked beautiful, like hair in the wind.

It started to rain.

"Miss Crosman is coming out again," said Mona.

"Don't let her talk you into going inside," I whispered.

"Why not?"

"Because that would mean Mom isn't really coming any minute."

"But she isn't," said Mona. "She's *working.*"

"Shhh! Miss Crosman is going to hear you."

"She's working! She's working! She's working!"

I put my hand over her mouth, but she licked it, and so I was wiping my hand on my wet dress when the front door opened.

"We're getting even *wetter,*" said Mona right away. "Wetter and wetter."

"Shall we all go in?" Miss Crosman pulled Mona to her feet. "Before you young ladies catch pneumonia? You've been out here an hour already."

"Were *freezing.*" Mona looked up at Miss Crosman. "Do

201

you have any hot chocolate? We're going to catch *pneumonia*."

"I'm not going in," I said. "My mother's coming any minute."

"Come on," said Mona. "Use your *noggin*."

"Any minute."

"Come on, Mona," Miss Crosman opened the door. "Shall we get you inside first?"

"See you in the hospital," said Mona as she went in. "See you in the hospital with *pneumonia*."

I stared out into the empty street. The rain was pricking me all over; I was cold; I wanted to go inside. I wanted to be able to let myself go inside. If Miss Crosman came out again, I decided, I would go in.

She came out with a blanket and the white umbrella.

I could not believe that I was actually holding the umbrella, opening it. It sprang up by itself as if it were alive, as if that were what it wanted to do — as if it belonged in my hands, above my head. I stared up at the network of silver spokes, then spun the umbrella around and around and around. It was so clean and white that it seemed to glow, to illuminate everything around it. "It's beautiful," I said.

Miss Crosman sat down next to me, on one end of the blanket. I moved the umbrella over so that it covered that too. I could feel the rain on my left shoulder and shivered. She put her arm around me.

"You poor, poor dear."

I knew that I was in store for another bolt of sympathy, and braced myself by staring up into the umbrella.

"You know, I very much wanted to have children when I was younger," she continued.

"You did?"

She stared at me a minute. Her face looked dry and crusty, like day-old frosting.

"I did. But then I never got married."

I twirled the umbrella around again.

"This is the most beautiful umbrella I have ever seen," I said. "Ever, in my whole life."

"Do you have an umbrella?"

"No. But my mother's going to get me one just like this for Christmas."

"Is she? I tell you what. You don't have to wait until Christmas. You can have this one."

"But this one belongs to Eugenie Roberts," I protested. "I have to give it back to her tomorrow in school."

"Who told you it belongs to Eugenie? It's not Eugenie's. It's mine. And now I'm giving it to you, so it's yours."

"It is?"

She hugged me tighter. "That's right. It's all yours."

"It's mine?" I didn't know what to say. "Mine?" Suddenly I was jumping up and down in the rain. "It's beautiful! Oh! It's beautiful!" I laughed.

Miss Crosman laughed too, even though she was getting all wet.

"Thank you, Miss Crosman. Thank you very much. Thanks a zillion. It's beautiful. It's *stupendous!*"

"You're quite welcome," she said.

"Thank you," I said again, but that didn't seem like enough. Suddenly I knew just what she wanted to hear. "I wish you were my mother."

Right away I felt bad.

"You shouldn't say that," she said, but her face was opening into a huge smile as the lights of my mother's car cautiously turned the corner. I quickly collapsed the umbrella and put it up my skirt, holding onto it from the outside, through the material.

"Mona!" I shouted into the house. "Mona! Hurry up! Mom's here! I told you she was coming!"

Then I ran away from Miss Crosman, down to the curb. Mona came tearing up to my side as my mother neared the house. We both backed up a few feet, so that in case she went onto the curb, she wouldn't run us over.

"But why didn't you go inside with Mona?" my mother asked on the way home. She had taken off her own coat to put over me, and had the heat on high.

"She wasn't using her noggin," said Mona, next to me in the back seat.

"I should call next time," said my mother. "I just don't like to say where I am."

That was when she finally told us that she was working as a check-out clerk in the A&P. She was supposed to be on the day shift, but the other employees were unreliable, and her boss had promised her a promotion if she would stay until the evening shift filled in.

For a moment no one said anything. Even Mona seemed to find the revelation disappointing.

"A promotion already!" she said, finally.

I listened to the windshield wipers.

"You're so quiet." My mother looked at me in the rear view mirror. "What's the matter?"

"I wish you would quit," I said after a moment.

She sighed. "The Chinese have a saying: one beam cannot hold the roof up."

"But Eugenie Roberts's father supports their family."

She sighed once more. "Eugenie Roberts's father is Eugenie Roberts's father," she said.

As we entered the downtown area, Mona started leaning hard against me every time the car turned right, trying to push me over. Remembering what I had said to Miss Crosman, I tried to maneuver the umbrella under my leg so she wouldn't feel it.

"What's under your skirt?" Mona wanted to know as we came to a traffic light. My mother, watching us in the rear view mirror again, rolled slowly to a stop.

"What's the matter?" she asked.

"There's something under her skirt?" said Mona, pulling at me. "Under her skirt?"

Meanwhile, a man crossing the street started to yell at us. "Who do you think you are, lady?" he said. "You're blocking the whole damn crosswalk."

We all froze. Other people walking by stopped to watch.

"Didn't you hear me?" he went on, starting to thump on the hood with his fist. "Don't you speak English?"

My mother began to back up, but the car behind us honked. Luckily, the light turned green right after that. She sighed in relief.

"What were you saying, Mona?" she asked.

We wouldn't have hit the car behind us that hard if he hadn't been moving too, but as it was our car bucked violently, throwing us all first back and then forward.

"Uh oh," said Mona when we stopped. *"Another* accident."

I was relieved to have attention diverted from the umbrella. Then I noticed my mother's head, tilted back onto the seat. Her eyes were closed.

"Mom!" I screamed. "Mom! Wake up!"

She opened her eyes. "Please don't yell," she said. "Enough people are going to yell already."

"I thought you were dead," I said, starting to cry. "I thought you were dead."

She turned around, looked at me intently, then put her hand to my forehead.

"Sick," she confirmed. "Some kind of sick is giving you crazy ideas."

As the man from the car behind us started tapping on the window, I moved the umbrella away from my leg. Then Mona and my mother were getting out of the car. I got out after them; and while everyone else was inspecting the damage we'd done, I threw the umbrella down a sewer.

Trudging,
or
Sari the Silent

ELLEN GRUBER GARVEY

The old people in a new world, the new people made out of the old,
that is the story that I mean to tell . . .
>   Gertrude Stein
>   *The Making of Americans*

We're taking her to a walk spe-
cialist. The pediatrician's afraid she's developing a slight
trudge. I've been getting worried.

And there are the clothes. It was fine the year everyone
was wearing shawls to see a nine-year-old in one — kind of
cute on her really, I liked that look — but that was three years
ago and no one at all is still wearing them, except Sari. Of
course she can always go down to Soho or the Village, the
way kids always do, and she'd still blend right in. Children
that age will often pick up some eccentricity or other, but this
doesn't seem the same.

Then last week, in the middle of the night, I heard a noise. Ronald wouldn't get up — he's never any help — and I got up. Not that there was really any reason. The doors and windows were locked of course, and there's the doorman and the elevator man besides, but I had to see what it was. The halls were empty. I walked to the pantry, and there was Sari — ironing, of all things, ironing! At first I thought, well she must need something for school tomorrow and worried about it so much she just had to get up and do it. I know just what that's like. Of course Sari's never been like that, but she's growing so fast, they change in so many ways, I wouldn't be surprised to see her becoming more of a young lady that way. One can't help feeling a bit flattered to see a child becoming a little like oneself. But then I saw what she was ironing — well that really threw me for a loop. She had out the sheets — not the regular Early American silk-screened ones, but those old white ones — and there they were, spread over the ironing board.

"But honey, those are no-iron sheets," I said. "And you don't have to do that. That's what we have the laundry down the street for. Why are you up now anyway? It's late."

"I was hungry," she said. I wasn't surprised. She'd only picked at her pork piperade at dinner. "I wanted some tea and toast. Do you think you could get some herring the next time you shop? I think I'd like some herring."

"Of course honey," I said. "What kind do you like, in that delicious cream sauce or in wine, or what?"

"Oh, just plain is fine. They probably have some smashed ones at the bottom of the barrel at the fish store that would be cheaper."

"You don't have to worry about that," I told her. She looked so shriveled in her bathrobe, I just wanted to sit there and feed her. Then I felt terrible — such a thought! Of course it's so much better that she's thin. Really, I'm glad for her. She doesn't have to work at it the way the rest of us do. Still, it wasn't right.

"I'll get you whatever you like best," I put my arm around her.

"No, no," she said. "That's all right. I'll manage. Whatever isn't any trouble for you. I don't have to have."

It was then, as she was on her way back to bed, that I noticed a kind of limp, maybe more of a shuffle — no, the pediatrician's right, it's a trudge, there's nothing else to call it.

"That's not a very attractive way to walk dear," I whispered down the hall — softly; if Ronald had slept through everything else he might as well sleep through this. Her little figure clumped along in the dark, leaning toward something at her side — almost protectively. "Try to be more careful."

"Why wouldn't I be careful?" she turned indignantly, and I saw the shopping bag swinging from her hand. "You think I'd want my bag to rip, to lose everything?

I couldn't help looking at the parquetry. "Elvira will be here in the morning, honey. Don't worry about the floor." I felt almost afraid to ask what was in the shopping bag, but of course it's just that kind of secrecy that can be so destructive to a healthy parent-child bond. "Is that something from school?" I asked.

"School?" she said. Were we going to have trouble with her hearing now on top of everything else? "No, not school." She seemed ill at ease, not quite frank.

"Just some scraps." That sounded more like her old self. Maybe she'd get out her collages again — she'd made the cutest little collages. We thought she had real talent — those cunning arrangements of designer labels from Ronald's old neckties, things like that.

"Let me see, dear."

The bag hit the floor with a thud. I've never seen Sari look so wistful as she looked at that bag. "From supper." She dragged it over.

It was the rye bread I'd put back in the kitchen after Elvira got back with a lovely fresh one; we're all very particular. "There was so much left over. Such a shame to waste it. Of course if you don't want me to have it — I wouldn't want to inconvenience you. I only thought —"

"You can have it, you can have anything you want. But why don't you tell me what you want? Just tell me what you want."

She looked up for a moment before she turned and trudged back down the hall to her room. The shawl nearly slipped, but she caught at it in time; the shopping bag on her arm weighted each step. If the walk specialist doesn't help, we don't know what to do.

Fierce Attachments (an excerpt)

VIVIAN GORNICK

We always walked, she and I. We don't always walk now. We don't always argue, either. We don't always do any of the things we always did. There is no always anymore. The fixed patterns are beginning to break up. This breakup has its own pleasures and surprises. In fact, surprise is now the key word between us. We cannot depend on change, but we can depend on surprise. However, we cannot always depend on surprise either. This keeps us on our toes.

I come to see her one night with an old friend of mine, a man who grew up with me, someone we've both known for thirty years. I say known advisedly. This man is something of a lunatic. An inspired lunatic, to be sure, but a lunatic nonetheless. He, like Davey Levinson, is educated in a vacuum, and he speaks a kind of imaginative gibberish. It is the only way he knows how to get through the ordinary anxiety of the ordinary day.

We are having coffee and cake. I am eating too much cake. I am, in fact, wolfing down the cake. My mother is getting crazy watching me. She cries, "Stop it! For God's sake, stop eating like that. Don't you care at all that you'll gain two pounds and hate yourself tomorrow? Where's your motivation?"

My friend, sitting at the table beside me, his head thrust forward and down and twisted to the side, looking at her like the madman that he is, starts going on nonsensically about motivation. "You know, of course, that motivation is life," he says. "Life itself. Taken from the Latin *motus,* it means to move, set in motion, engage . . ."

My mother looks at him. I can see in her face that she does not understand the construction of these sentences. She feels put down: if she doesn't understand something she is being told she is stupid. Her expression becomes one of glittering scorn. "You think you're telling me something I don't know?" she says. "You think I was born yesterday?" No surprise here.

One week later I'm sitting in her apartment drinking tea with her, and from out of nowhere she says to me, "So tell me about your abortion." She knows I had an abortion when I was thirty, but she has never referred to it. I, in turn, know she had three abortions during the Depression, but I never mention them, either. Now, suddenly . . . Her face is unreadable. I don't know what has stirred the inquiry and I don't know what to tell her. Should I tell her the truth or . . .? What the hell. The truth. "I had an abortion with my legs up against the wall in an apartment on West Eighty-eighth Street, with Demerol injected into my veins by a doctor whose consulting room was the corner of Fifty-eighth Street and Tenth Avenue." She nods at me as I speak, as though these details are familiar, even expected. Then she says, "I had mine in the basement of a Greenwich Village nightclub, for ten dollars, with a doctor who half the time when you woke up you were holding his penis in your hand." I look at her with admiration. She has

211

matched me clause for clause, and raised the ante with each one. We both burst out laughing at the same moment. Surprise.

Yet another night I am sitting at her table and we are talking of the time she went to work when I was eight years old. This is a story I never tire of hearing.

"What made you decide to do it, Ma? I mean, why that time rather than any other?"

"I always wanted to work, always. God, how I loved having my own money in my pocket! It was the middle of the war, you threw a stone you got seven jobs, I couldn't resist."

"So what did you do?"

"I read the want ads one morning and I got dressed, took the subway downtown, and applied for a job. In ten minutes I had it. What was the name of that company? I've forgotten it now."

"Angelica Uniform Company," I instantly supply.

"You remember!" She smiles beatifically at me. "Look at that. She remembers. I can't remember. She remembers."

"I am the repository of your life now, Ma."

"Yes, you are, you are. Let's see now. Where were we?"

"You went downtown and got the job."

"Yes. So I came home and told Papa, 'I have a job.'"

"How did he respond?"

"Badly. Very badly. He didn't want me to work. He said, 'No other wife in the neighborhood works, why should you work.' I said, 'I don't care what any other wife in the neighborhood does, I want to work.'" She stares into this memory, shaking her head. Her voice falters. "But it was no good, no good. I didn't last long."

"Eight months," I say.

"Yes, eight months."

"Why, Ma? Why only eight months?"

"Papa was miserable. He kept saying to me, 'The children need you.'"

"That was silly," I interrupt. "I remember being *excited*

that you were working. I loved having a key around my neck, and rushing home every afternoon to do things that made it easier for you."

"Then he said, 'You're losing weight.'"

"You were twenty pounds overweight. It was *great* that you were losing weight."

"What can I tell you?" she says to me. "Either you were going to make a hell in the house or you were going to be happy. I wanted to be happy. He didn't want me to work. I stopped working."

We are quiet together for a while. Then I say, "Ma, if it was now, and Papa said he didn't want you to work, what would you do?"

She looks at me for a long moment. She is eighty years old. Her eyes are dim, her hair is white, her body is frail. She takes a swallow of tea, puts down the cup, and says calmly, "I'd tell him to go fuck himself."

Real surprise.

We're in the Lincoln Center library for a Saturday afternoon concert. We've arrived late and all the seats are taken. We stand in the darkened auditorium leaning against the wall. I start to worry. I know my mother cannot stand for two and a half hours. "Let's go," I whisper to her. "Sh-h-h," she says, pushing the air away with her hand. I look around. In the aisle seat next to me is a little boy, tossing about on his seat. Beside him his young mother. Next to her another little boy, and next to him the husband and father. The woman lifts the little boy in the aisle seat onto her lap and motions my mother to sit down. My mother leans over, gives the woman her most brilliant smile, and says coyly, "When you'll be eighty, and you'll want a seat at a concert, I'll come back and give you one." The woman is charmed. She turns to her husband to share her pleasure. Nothing doing. He stares balefully at my mother. Here is one Jewish son who hasn't forgotten. His response pulls me up short, reminds me of how seductive my mother has always been, how unwilling she is to part with this oldest trick of the trade, how dangerous and untrustworthy is this charm of hers.

On and on it goes. My apartment is being painted. I spend two nights on her couch. Whenever I sleep over I like to make the coffee in the morning, because she has gotten used to weak coffee and I like mine strong. Meanwhile, she has become convinced that her weak coffee is the correct way to make coffee, and although she has said to me, "All right, you don't like my coffee, make it yourself," she stands over me in the kitchen and directs me to make it as she makes it.

"It's enough already," she says as I spoon coffee into the pot.

"No, it's not," I say.

"It *is*. For God's sake, enough!"

"Look for yourself, Ma. See how far short of the measuring line it is?"

She looks. The evidence is indisputable. There is not enough coffee in the pot. She turns away from me, the flat edge of her hand cutting the air in that familiar motion of dismissal.

"Ah, leave me alone," she says in deep trembling disgust.

I stare at her retreating back. That dismissiveness of hers: it will be the last thing to go. In fact, it will never go. It is the emblem of her speech, the idiom of her being, that which establishes her in her own eyes. The dismissal of others is to her the struggle to rise from the beasts, to make distinctions, to know the right and the wrong of a thing, to not think it unimportant, ever, that the point be made. Suddenly her life presses on my heart.

Mothers, Daughters

MARGARET ERHART

Our mother was tall and slender, with cool hands that stroked the back of a fever.

She outdid herself at Christmas.

She recorded the height of her two children twice a year on the back of the bathroom door.

Our mother was tall and slender wearing polo coats and knee boots to autumn parades.

Her colors were browns and forest greens. White in the summer.

She tanned easily. She was tan all year without trying.

She read books to her children and introduced them to the taste of kidneys cooked in wine, salmon in cream sauce.

My sister is younger. She sits at the butcher block table in the kitchen and tells my mother she doesn't want to eat. My mother says only, "You will be hungry."

Toria hates her in that moment. She pushes away from the table and leaves the kitchen.

That isn't the beginning of the story.

No. But it's part of the story.

We are all part of the story. Toria. My mother. Myself.

We collected photographs for the leather-covered album. Every November we sat up for days and nights filling the empty pages of the album.

The three of us.

My mother made tea. If it was cold we lit the fire.

Every few years there would be a new album. I was fifteen before I looked through the oldest album. Toria was twelve.

Our mother brought it to us where we sat on the floor of the living room. The leather was spotted with age. The corners were frayed.

"There are pictures of your father in here," she said. And that was all she said.

He was a strong man with sympathetic eyes.

Mother went to make tea.

"What are the wings for?" Toria asked.

"He was a pilot," I said. "Pilots wear little wings above their heart to help them fly."

"I don't believe you," she said.

And mother came with the tea.

Toria turned to the front of the album. "Who's this?" she said. "It looks like me."

Mother laughed. "It's your mother," she said.

Toria stared at the photograph. She pulled up the corners that held it in the album.

"That's me," she said. "That's got to be me. It looks just like me."

It looked just like her. Wide eyes — eyes too big for the face they rested in. Full cheeks casting two diagonal shadows across the nose. A question mark in each corner of the mouth. The girl in the photograph sat at the shallow end of an empty swimming pool. Leaves stuck to her hair. Leaves covered the bottom of the swimming pool. She looked directly at the camera.

"But I don't remember that swimming pool," said Toria.

"It was in Litchfield, Connecticut," Mother said, "at the home of one of my mother's friends. Late October."

Toria stares at her as she has been staring at the photograph.

"I don't believe you," she says, and she takes the photograph out and closes the album.

We never talked about my father.

Our mother did not keep memories in little boxes on her bureau.

No cufflinks, tie clasps.

Not the little wings.

The little wings disappeared with him somewhere in the ocean between San Francisco and Honolulu.

That is all I know of my father.

I was three. Toria was a lump in my mother's belly.

She was born a week after the funeral with the cord around her neck and her eyes wide open.

Toria and I shared a bedroom. It had a long mirror on the back of the door. She never looked in the mirror until she was twelve and then she looked in it all the time.

But she didn't look at her reflection.

She looked beyond her reflection.

She looked past the eyes that looked back at her. Eyes that were always too big for their face.

"I'm flat," she said.

I said "What?"

"I'm flat. In the mirror I'm flat. I like it."

She touched her hands to her face and let them fall slowly down across her body. I noticed the beginning of a curve at her hips. Her body was fuller. Her face was fuller.

"I'd like to be flat and light as air," she said.

"You would blow away," I said.

She shook her head. "No," she said, "I would fly away. There's a difference."

For Toria there was a difference.

For Mother there was no difference.

I tried to understand both sides and feel at times that I have understood neither.

After she sees the old photograph of Mother and confuses it with herself Toria sits at the butcher block table and says she doesn't want to eat.

"You will be hungry," Mother says and she watches her daughter run out of the kitchen.

"I don't want to eat," says Toria the next morning at breakfast.

And again at lunch.

And dinner.

"I don't want to eat," she says for a week.

And Mother says nothing.

She fills my plate and her plate and puts Toria's plate in the oven. She turns the oven on low. She leaves the food on the stove on low. And only then does she sit down to eat.

We sit across from each other and Toria sits at the end of the table drinking water. She says nothing. Mother and I talk around her because she tells us with her eyes that she doesn't want to be part. She wants to brush the edge with her glass of water but she doesn't want to be part.

For a week this goes on.

For a week, and then Mother cries, and that's what Toria is waiting for. It gives her strength to continue.

Two weeks before Christmas I lay in bed with the German measles. I was glad to get the German measles because everyone said if you got them during pregnancy you would give birth to a one-armed child, or a child with no legs, or two heads. I was glad to get the German measles over with.

I was told later that you never get the German measles over with. You get them again and again. There will always be that chance that you give birth to a monster.

I lay in Mother's bed because there she could hear me from the kitchen. She was making Indian pudding that morning and her cool hands on my forehead smelled of dark molasses.

The telephone rang.

I watched Mother's face sag with new lines of worry. Between her eyes. Around her eyes. Like fences.

"Yes," she said, "I'll come right away."

She hung up the telephone.

"Your sister is in the hospital," she said. She stroked my hair. It was damp with fever. "Where do you hurt?"

I shook my head. "Nowhere," I said. "Go see Toria. I'll be fine."

Mother took her coat and stood in the doorway.

"There's Indian pudding," she said. "It's still hot."

I was in bed with the German measles but the school nurse told me about it later. She had tried to tell my mother in the hospital but Mother wasn't interested. She didn't care how it had happened. It had happened.

I don't think the new lines around her eyes had much to do with worry. I think they had more to do with regret. The greatest fault my mother recognized in anyone was the failure to pay attention.

With Toria she felt she had not paid attention.

Toria stands on the top step of the stage in the school assembly hall. She is dressed in a black choir robe. She sings alto. The music teacher leads them through the first piece and the other teachers and students applaud. They begin the second piece and Toria starts to rock back and forth. She drops her music. The black choir robe crumples. She falls forward down the steps and lands unconscious at the bottom step.

The assembly is dismissed.

The school nurse opens a bottle of smelling salts under Toria's nose. She comes to for a moment, then falls unconscious again.

"Someone call an ambulance," says the nurse.

The music teacher says, "Someone help me get her out of this choir robe. The damn things are too hot."

Mother outdid herself at Christmas.

I helped her wrap packages and tie ribbons.

The taxi stopped outside the door marked "Visitors" and Mother and I unloaded the boxes. Inside the hospital we rode the elevator to the seventh floor and Mother led the way down the hallway to a door on the left.

The last door on the left.

Room seven-hundred.

"Come in," said Toria. I hadn't seen her since the last morning she left for school, when I had the German measles.

"Your eyes have grown," I said.

She said, "I know."

They frightened me those eyes.

Mother leaned across the intravenous tubes to kiss her.

Her face had died around those eyes.

Mother said, "We brought you Christmas."

"I know," she said.

I piled the boxes on the bed and sat down next to them. Mother pulled a chair from the corner. We sat looking at the boxes and at the tubes running up the sleeve of Toria's hospital pajamas.

"No one brought you flowers," I said.

Toria's mouth tightened in a little smile.

"Mother brought me flowers," she said, "but they died."

"Let's open presents," Mother said. "There are lots of

presents."

I watched my sister and my mother open presents on the bed in room seven-hundred. That was my fifteenth Christmas. Toria's twelfth. Mother's thirty-ninth. We spent it together on the seventh floor of a hospital with a view across the river to New Jersey, in a room without flowers or television. Just a gray intravenous bottle dripping food into my emaciated sister.

My sister who had become as flat as her image in the mirror.

And as lifeless.

My sister who had become light as air.

"You've grown some wings," I said to her. I pointed to the back of her pajamas where her shoulder blades pressed against the cotton.

Her mouth tightened again. Her new smile.

"I like them," she said.

"When's your first flight?"

She pointed to the intravenous bottle above her head. "As soon as they unhook me," she said.

"Where will you go?"

"Out," she said, "and up. They're going to put bars on the window but I think I can squeeze through."

Mother was uncomfortable. "There are more presents, Toria," she said.

But Toria was tired of opening presents. She was tired of notepaper with her name in block letters at the top, and matching envelopes. She was tired of children in books who did great things that never really happened. Animals that talked. Radios that played the same songs at the same time all across the city.

She was tired and that frightened her.

"I want you to go," she said.

Another small moment of hate.

The lines wrinkled around Mother's eyes.

In the elevator I held her hand and in the taxi I held her hand. She fixed hot soup at home and we ate on the floor of the living room in front of the fire. Outside it snowed eighteen inches, paralyzing the city.

"What did she mean 'They're going to put bars on the window'?"

Mother looked at me across the table.

"They're going to put bars on the window of her room," she said, "so she can't fall out."

"Or fly out," I said.

"Or jump out. They're afraid she might jump out."

"Who's 'they'?"

"The doctors," she said. "The psychiatrists."

"She's seeing psychiatrists?" I said.

"They're seeing her."

Mother talked about those first two weeks in the hospital. Toria had been admitted with a severe case of malnutrition. Mother had filled out the proper forms and answered the doctor's questions.

"When was the last time your daughter took food into her body?"

Mother had answered "I don't know."

"When was the last time you saw her eat?"

Mother hesitated. "November twenty-ninth," she said. "She ate lunch. Chicken salad."

"That was eleven days ago," said the doctor.

"No," said Mother, "twelve."

The doctor didn't want to use the intravenous unless absolutely necessary. He said, "We don't want her to become dependent on a bottle."

After the second day in the hospital Toria was still refusing food. The flesh on her face had disappeared. Her body had disappeared.

Mother cried in the taxi between the hospital and home.

On the third day a clean nurse wheeled the intravenous into position above Toria's bed and hooked her up to it. The little arm jumped with new life and the nurse wrapped white tape around the tubes to anchor them in place.

"She will be seeing a psychiatrist," the doctor told Mother.

She nodded.

"He is a fine doctor."

She wished she had paid attention.

"He works only with children."

Mother said, "Is she a child?"

Mother said, "I don't think she's a child."

She tells me all this at the kitchen table. The food on our plates is cold. Another foot of snow is expected in the city.

Toria had a dream about snow.

She called it a nightmare.

"There are drifts," she said. "Deep drifts of snow through the woods. I'm alone. There's no path. I'm moving between the trees."

Toria pulled the hospital blanket around her and leaned forward on the bed.

"You're moving between the trees," I said.

"Yes, I'm moving between the trees and stopping to look back at my tracks in the snow. But they're not mine. The footprints aren't mine. They're deeper, heavier. I keep walking. And stopping. And looking back. And then they're ahead of me too. The same tracks, where there weren't tracks before. These footprints in the woods."

That was the night after they unhooked the intravenous. A week before she came home.

I heard Toria talk about the dream only once after that and she told it as if it had really happened.

Mother bought fresh flowers. Flowers in every room.

Toria came home in the afternoon and changed into clean

223

pajamas. She sat in her bed and Mother brought hot malted milk on the folding tray.

"What was he like?" she asked.

Mother looked at her. "What was who like?"

"My father."

Mother looked away.

Across miles.

Years.

She didn't remember.

She had forgotten.

She should have paid attention.

Why hadn't she paid attention?

Toria stands with her back to the mirror staring at the photograph.

"I know that's not me," she says. "I don't look like that."

"It's Mother," I say. "In Litchfield, Connecticut."

She turns to the mirror. "I just don't look like that."

Only the eyes in the photograph are the eyes in the mirror. The rest is gone. The little breasts, the hips. The fullness is gone. Her bones show like islands under the skin.

Toria watches her body in the mirror. She runs her fingers down the mirror, touching her reflection.

She doesn't look beyond her reflection.

She looks directly at it.

For the first time in her life she looks directly at it.

Mama's Life:
A Long Distance
Monologue

RACHEL GUIDO deVRIES

If only he had Alzheimer's, I could
explain his moods. But he doesn't, the doctor told me when
I went for my heart check-up. Yes, he changed my pills, I only
take one now, in the morning, before I had to take one at night
too. But he said he won't give your father any more Valium,
but there's a new pill, one you take at night and you wake up
feeling terrific. I told your father about it, but so far he hasn't
gone. But the doctor was nice, he put his hand on my shoulder
and said, Mrs. Zingarelli, you don't have to worry about that,
he doesn't have Alzheimer's. In a way, I almost wish he did,
then there would at least be a reason. He's cranky, crankier
than usual, not just cranky, he's nasty all the time. Nothing
pleases him.

I told the doctor I'm getting some exercise, but I exaggerated a little, I told him I walk Fritz every morning but I really
don't, I just walk to the mailbox with him. I bowl two times
a week, and I also told him I swim once in a while. He wanted

to know how many laps. I asked him what he meant, I didn't know what laps were in swimming. He told me and I laughed, I told him I just doggy paddle in the pool. Then he laughed, and he told me to tell your father to come in the office and talk to him, just as a friend. He told me my daughter the nurse, that's you, could call him any time and ask whatever questions you want. Or I could call you and ask you questions and you could call him and ask him the right way, I'm never sure what to ask.

Wait, no your father's not here, but he is on the other phone, hold on a minute, honey.

Okay, I'm back. No he didn't want nothing special, he was just checking in before he comes in. No, we're not too busy now, the snow birds won't start coming for another month or so, but we're doin' alright. What's your zip code again, I think I sent your birthday card to the wrong place, it's got money in it too. How do you spell your last name again, I can never remember it all these years, since you married that Dutchman. I heard his mother's sick, I sent her a card, a cute little get well card, maybe she'll send a little thank you card when she gets it.

Well, you've both changed, he's middle aged now. So are you. You're getting your period? Enjoy it, you don't have that many left, ha ha. I don't do that stuff any more. I don't even remember it. Me and you father are becoming Jai-Lai nuts, we win once in a while. Well, at least we're a little more active than we were, we're doin' more things now instead of just watching that TV. You know your father bought that big one, jeez, it's huge, ridiculous. How big is it? I think it's about 45 inches, he likes it for football. But even that don't please him, he can't figure out how to work it with the satellite dish, and then that friggin' cable, we have too many remote controls. Uncle Phil came over last week and screwed it all up. Your father almost had a stroke over it, I told him, Nick, relax, it's just a TV.

Oh, jeez, wait a minute, honey, it's your father again on the other line. We got a new cleaning lady and she's a pain in the ass, she's a nice lady, but she don't do right. Ciel had it perfect before she left, she knew where everything was. I wish she'd come back, but you know that guy she's married to is a weirdo, she thinks he's fooling around. No, not another woman, she thinks he's doin' it with guys. Holy Christ! Least I never had to worry about that with your father, he just went for *putonas*. No more though, he's finally too old. Maybe that's why he's so cranky, ha ha. We don't fool around any more, I told you that. I don't like it. We tried once, at this little cottage that Gus and Millie own, right on the bay. It was so cute, and I thought maybe, but he was in a mood that night, real nasty. I think he can't, you know, he can't do it no more. He went to the last doctor, that Indian one, and that one told him he could give him this little thing, like a stick or something, to put in when he wanted to. Your father thought he was crazy, he said "Ya know what that sonofabitch tol' me? He wanted to cut the ole' trolley car, put a stick in it." Your father and me got a laugh out of that one. At least he still has a sense of humor, when he uses it. But he don't use it that much lately. I don't know what's the matter with him. Plus he can't hear, but he won't get a hearing aid, and he acts like it's everybody's fault, like we're deliberately talking so he can't hear, he's always going, "what, what, huh," in that nasty tone he gets. Yeah, I know he did that when you were here last time, but he can't help it, honey, he can't hear.

Oh, for Christ's sake, there he is again on the other phone. He's driving me crazy, calls a million times before he comes in. Wait a minute, honey.

Okay, I'm back. He wants Nicky, he wants him to call the liquor salesman, I don't know why he just can't tell him when he gets here, that's what I mean, he creates his own problems. "Call your son," he said to me, like he does when he wants to act like Nicky's not like him, which he isn't thank God. But listen, honey, I gotta brush you off. Why? Because I have to call Nicky and wake him up, you know how your brother Nicky likes to sleep late. Your father thinks he's on his way in here, but I know he's still sleeping. Yes, at 10 in the morning, with a business to run. What can I tell you, honey, you know some things never change. One's lazy as sin, the other, your father, is cranky. Nasty. That's why I want to call Nicky right away, so he'll be here, looking bright-eyed and bushy-tailed when your father gets here.

I love you too, honey. Don't worry about nothing. We're all fine down here. At least we know your father don't have Alzheimer's. Call me next week, I'll keep you posted.

Mother

GRACE PALEY

One day I was listening to the AM radio. I heard a song: "Oh, I Long to See My Mother in the Doorway." By God! I said, I understand that song. I have often longed to see my mother in the doorway. As a matter of fact, she did stand frequently in various doorways looking at me. She stood one day, just so, at the front door, the darkness of the hallway behind her. It was New Year's Day. She said sadly, If you come home at 4 a.m. when you're seventeen, what time will you come home when you're twenty? She asked this question without humor or meanness. She had begun her worried preparations for death. She would not be present, she thought, when I was twenty. So she wondered.

Another time she stood in the doorway of my room. I had just issued a political manifesto attacking the family's position on the Soviet Union. She said, Go to sleep for godsakes, you damn fool, you and your Communist ideas. We saw them already, Papa and me, in 1905. We guessed it all.

At the door of the kitchen she said, You never finish your lunch. You run around senselessly. What will become of you?

Then she died.

Naturally for the rest of my life I longed to see her, not only in doorways, in a great number of places — in the dining room with my aunts, at the window looking up and down the block, in the country garden among zinnias and marigolds, in the living room with my father.

They sat in comfortable leather chairs. They were listening to Mozart. They looked at one another amazed. It seemed to them that they'd just come over on the boat. They'd just learned the first English words. It seemed to them that he had just proudly handed in a 100 percent correct exam to the American anatomy professor. It seemed as though she'd just quit the shop for the kitchen.

I wish I could see her in the doorway of the living room.

She stood there a minute. Then she sat beside him. They owned an expensive record player. They were listening to Bach. She said to him, Talk to me a little. We don't talk so much anymore.

I'm tired, he said. Can't you see? I saw maybe thirty people today. All sick, all talk talk talk talk. Listen to the music, he said. I believe you once had perfect pitch. I'm tired, he said.

Then she died.

The Leap

LOUISE ERDRICH

My mother is the surviving half of a blindfold trapeze act, not a fact I think about much even now that she is sightless, the result of encroaching and stubborn cataracts. She walks slowly through her house here in New Hampshire, lightly touching her way along walls and running her hands over knickknacks, books, the drift of a grown child's belongings and castoffs. She has never upset an object or as much as brushed a magazine onto the floor. She has never lost her balance or bumped into a closet door left carelessly open.

It has occurred to me that the catlike precision of her movements in old age might be the result of her early training, but she shows so little of the drama or flair one might expect from a performer that I tend to forget the Flying Avalons. She has kept no sequined costume, no photographs, no fliers or posters from that part of her youth. I would, in fact, tend to think that all memory of double somersaults and heart-stopping catches had left her arms and legs were it not for the fact that sometimes, as I sit sewing in the room of the rebuilt house in which I slept as a child, I hear the crackle, catch a whiff of smoke from the stove downstairs, and suddenly the room goes dark, the stitches burn beneath my fingers, and I am sewing with a needle of hot silver, a thread of fire.

I owe her my existence three times. The first was when she saved herself. In the town square a replica tent pole, cracked and splintered, now stands cast in concrete. It commemorates the disaster that put our town smack on the front page of the Boston and New York tabloids. It is from those old newspapers, now historical records, that I get my information. Not from my mother, Anna of the Flying Avalons, nor from any of her in-laws, nor certainly from the other half of her particular act, Harold Avalon, her first husband. In one news account it says, "The day was mildly overcast, but nothing in the air or temperature gave any hint of the sudden force with which the deadly gale would strike."

I have lived in the West, where you can see the weather coming for miles, and it is true that out here we are at something of a disadvantage. When extremes of temperature collide, a hot and cold front, winds generate instantaneously behind a hill and crash upon you without warning. That, I think, was the likely situation on that day in June. People probably commented on the pleasant air, grateful that no hot sun beat upon the striped tent that stretched over the entire center green. They bought their tickets and surrendered them in anticipation. They sat. They ate carmelized popcorn and roasted peanuts. There was time, before the storm, for three acts. The White Arabians of Ali-Khazar rose on their hind legs and waltzed. The Mysterious Bernie folded himself into a painted cracker tin, and the Lady of the Mists made herself appear and disappear in surprising places. As the clouds gathered outside, unnoticed, the ringmaster cracked his whip, shouted his introduction, and pointed to the ceiling of the tent, where the Flying Avalons were perched.

They loved to drop gracefully from nowhere, like two sparkling birds, and blow kisses as they threw off their plumed helmets and high-collared capes. They laughed and flirted openly as they beat their way up again on the trapeze bars. In the final vignette of their act, they actually would kiss in midair, pausing, almost hovering as they swooped past one another. On the ground, between bows, Harry Avalon would skip quickly to the front rows and point out the smear of my mother's lipstick, just off the edge of his mouth. They made a romantic pair all right, especially in the blindfold sequence.

That afternoon, as the anticipation increased, as Mr. and Mrs. Avalon tied sparkling strips of cloth onto each other's face and as they puckered their lips in mock kisses, lips destined "never again to meet," as one long breathless article put it, the wind rose, miles off, wrapped itself into a cone, and howled. There came a rumble of electrical energy, drowned out by the sudden roll of drums. One detail not mentioned by the press, perhaps unknown — Anna was pregnant at the time, seven months and hardly showing, her stomach muscles were that strong. It seems incredible that she would work high above the ground when any fall could be so dangerous, but the explanation — I know from watching her go blind — is that my mother lives comfortably in extreme elements. She is one with the constant dark now, just as the air was her home, familiar to her, safe, before the storm that afternoon.

From opposite ends of the tent they waved, blind and smiling, to the crowd below. The ringmaster removed his hat and called for silence, so that the two above could concentrate. They rubbed their hands in chalky powder, then Harry launched himself and swung, once, twice, in huge calibrated beats across space. He hung from his knees and on the third swing stretched wide his arms, held his hands out to receive his pregnant wife as she dove from her shining bar.

It was while the two were in midair, their hands about to

meet, that lightning struck the main pole and sizzled down the guy wires, filling the air with a blue radiance that Harry Avalon must certainly have seen through the cloth of his blindfold as the tent buckled and the edifice toppled him forward, the swing continuing and not returning in its sweep, and Harry going down, down into the crowd with his last thought, perhaps, just a prickle of surprise at his empty hands.

My mother once said that I'd be amazed at how many things a person can do within the act of falling. Perhaps, at the time, she was teaching me to dive off a board at the town pool, for I associate the idea with midair somersaults. But I also think she meant that even in that awful doomed second one could think, for she certainly did. When her hands did not meet her husband's, my mother tore her blindfold away. As he swept past her on the wrong side, she could have grasped his ankle, the toe-end of his tights, and gone down clutching him. Instead, she changed direction. Her body twisted toward a heavy wire and she managed to hang on to the braided metal, still hot from the lightning strike. Her palms were burned so terribly that once healed they bore no lines, only the blank scar tissue of a quieter future. She was lowered, gently, to the sawdust ring just underneath the dome of the canvas roof, which did not entirely settle but was held up on one end and jabbed through, torn, and still on fire in places from the giant spark, though rain and men's jackets soon put that out.

Three people died, but except for her hands my mother was not seriously harmed until an overeager rescuer broke her arm in extricating her and also, in the process, collapsed a portion of the tent bearing a huge buckle that knocked her unconscious. She was taken to the town hospital, and there she must have hemorrhaged, for they kept her, confined to her bed, a month and a half before her baby was born without life.

Harry Avalon had wanted to be buried in the circus cemetery next to the original Avalon, his uncle, so she sent him back with his brothers. The child, however, is buried around the corner, beyond this house and just down the highway. Sometimes I used to walk there just to sit. She was a girl, but I rarely thought of her as a sister or even as a separate person really. I suppose you could call it the ego-centrism of a child, of all young children, but I considered her a less finished version of myself.

When the snow falls, throwing shadows among the stones, I can easily pick hers out from the road, for it is bigger than the others and in the shape of a lamb at rest, its legs curled beneath. The carved lamb looms larger as the years pass, though it is probably only my eyes, the vision shifting, as what is close to me blurs and distances sharpen. In odd moments, I think it is the edge drawing near, the edge of everything, the unseen horizon we do not really speak of in the eastern woods. And it also seems to me, although this is probably an idle fantasy, that the statue is growing more sharply etched, as if, instead of weathering itself into a porous mass, it is hardening on the hillside with each snow-fall, perfecting itself.

It was during her confinement in the hospital that my mother met my father. He was called in to look at the set of her arm, which was complicated. He stayed, sitting at her bedside, for he was something of an armchair traveler and had spent his war quietly, at an air force training grounds, where he became a specialist in arms and legs broken during parachute training exercises. Anna Avalon had been to many of the places he longed to visit — Venice, Rome, Mexico, all through France and Spain. She had no family of her own and was taken in by the Avalons, trained to perform from a very young age. They toured Europe before the war, then based themselves in New York. She was illiterate.

It was in the hospital that she finally learned to read and write, as a way of overcoming the boredom and depression of those weeks, and it was my father who insisted on teaching her. In return for stories of her adventures, he graded her first exercises. He bought her her first book, and over her bold letters, which the pale guides of the penmanship pads could not contain, they fell in love.

I wonder if my father calculated the exchange he offered: one form of flight for another. For after that, and for as long as I can remember, my mother has never been without a book. Until now, that is, and it remains the greatest difficulty of her blindness. Since my father's recent death, there is no one to read to her, which is why I returned, in fact, from my failed life where the land is flat. I came home to read to my mother, to read out loud, to read long into the dark if I must, to read all night.

Once my father and mother married, they moved onto the old farm he had inherited but didn't care much for. Though he'd been thinking of moving to a larger city, he settled down and broadened his practice in this valley. It still seems odd to me, when they could have gone anywhere else, that they chose to stay in the town where the disaster had occurred, and which my father in the first place had found so constricting. It was my mother who insisted upon it, after her child did not survive. And then, too, she loved the sagging farmhouse with its scrap of what was left of a vast acreage of woods and hidden hay fields that stretched to the game park.

I owe my existence, the second time then, to the two of them and the hospital that brought them together. That is the debt we take for granted since none of us asks for life. It is only once we have it that we hang on so dearly.

I was seven the year the house caught fire, probably from standing ash. It can rekindle, and my father, forgetful around the house and perpetually exhausted from night hours on call, often emptied what he thought were ashes from cold stoves into wooden or cardboard containers. The fire could have started from a flaming box, or perhaps a buildup of creosote inside the chimney was the culprit. It started right around the stove, and the heart of the house was gutted. The baby-sitter, fallen asleep in my father's den on the first floor, woke to find the stairway to my upstairs room cut off by flames. She used the phone, then ran outside to stand beneath my window.

When my parents arrived, the town volunteers had drawn water from the fire pond and were spraying the outside of the house, preparing to go inside after me, not knowing at the time that there was only one staircase and that it was lost. On the other side of the house, the superannuated extension ladder broke in half. Perhaps the clatter of it falling against the walls woke me, for I'd been asleep up to that point.

As soon as I awakened, in the small room that I now use for sewing, I smelled the smoke. I followed things by the letter then, was good at memorizing instructions, and so I did exactly what I was taught in the second-grade home fire drill. I got up, I touched the back of my door before opening it. Finding it hot, I left it closed and stuffed my rolled-up rug beneath the crack. I did not hide under my bed or crawl into my closet. I put on my flannel robe, and then I sat down to wait.

Outside, my mother stood below my dark window and saw clearly that there was no rescue. Flames had pierced one side wall, and the glare of the fire lighted the massive limbs and trunk of the vigorous old elm that had probably been planted the year the house was built, a hundred years ago at least. No leaf touched the wall, and just one thin branch scraped the roof. From below, it looked as though even a squirrel would have had trouble jumping from the tree onto the house, for the breadth of that small branch was no bigger than my mother's wrist.

Standing there, beside Father, who was preparing to rush back around to the front of the house, my mother asked him to unzip her dress. When he wouldn't be bothered, she made him understand. He couldn't make his hands work, so she finally tore it off and stood there in her pearls and stockings.

She directed one of the men to lean the broken half of the extension ladder up against the trunk of the tree. In surprise, he complied. She ascended. She vanished. Then she could be seen among the leafless branches of late November as she made her way up and, along her stomach, inched the length of a bough that curved above the branch that brushed the roof.

Once there, swaying, she stood and balanced. There were plenty of people in the crowd and many who still remember, or think they do, my mother's leap through the ice-dark air toward that thinnest extension, and how she broke the branch falling so that it cracked in her hands, cracked louder than the flames as she vaulted with it toward the edge of the roof, and how it hurtled down end over end without her, and their eyes went up, again, to see where she had flown.

I didn't see her leap through air, only heard the sudden thump and looked out my window. She was hanging by the backs of her heels from the new gutter we had put in that year, and she was smiling. I was not surprised to see her, she was so matter-of-fact. She tapped on the window. I remember how she did it, too. It was the friendliest tap, a bit tentative, as if she was afraid she had arrived too early at a friend's house. Then she gestured at the latch, and when I opened the window she told me to raise it wider and prop it up with the stick so it wouldn't crush her fingers. She swung down, caught the ledge, and crawled through the opening. Once she was in my room, I realized she had on only underclothing, a bra of the heavy stitched cotton women used to wear and step-in, lace-trimmed drawers. I remember feeling light-headed, of course, terribly relieved, and then embarrassed for her to be seen by the crowd undressed.

I was still embarrassed as we flew out the window, toward earth, me in her lap, her toes pointed as we skimmed toward the painted target of the fire fighter's net.

I know that she's right. I knew it even then. As you fall there is time to think. Curled as I was, against her stomach, I was not startled by the cries of the crowd or the looming faces. The wind roared and beat its hot breath at our back, the flames whistled. I slowly wondered what would happen if we missed the circle or bounced out of it. Then I wrapped my hands around my mother's hands. I felt the brush of her lips and heard the beat of her heart in my ears, loud as thunder, long as the roll of drums.

Contributors' Notes

June Arnold was born in Greenville, South Carolina in 1926 and she died in 1982. She was the co-founder of Daughters, Inc., one of the first lesbian/feminist publishing companies in the United States. She is the author of *Applesauce, The Cook and the Carpenter, Sister Gin* and *Baby Houston.*

Carol Ascher was born in Cleveland, Ohio, three months after her parents came to this country in 1941. She now lives in New York and divides her time between writing fiction and analyzing issues in urban education. *The Flood* is her most recent novel.

Maureen Brady is the author of a collection of short stories, *The Question She Put to Herself,* and two novels, *Give Me Your Good Ear* and *Folly.* Her third novel, *Rocking Bone Hollow,* was recently completed.

Kim Chernin was born in the Bronx in 1940. She is the author of *The Obsession: Reflections on the Tyranny of Slenderness; Reinventing Eve: Modern Woman in Search of Herself; The Hungry Self: Women, Eating, and Identity; The Flame Bearers; In My Mother's House: A Daughter's Story;* and *Sex and Other Sacred Games: Love, Desire, Power and Possession* (co-authored with Renate Stendhal).

Rachel Guido DeVries was born in 1947 and is a second generation Italian-American. A poet and novelist, she co-founded and directs The Community Writers' Project, Inc., in Syracuse, New York. Her novel, *Tender Warriors,* was published in 1986; she is the fiction editor of *Ikon;* her work has appeared most recently in *Yellow Silk, Voices in Italian Americana, Sinister Wisdom* and *My Father's Daughter.*

Louise Erdrich was born in 1954 and grew up in North Dakota. She is the author of two volumes of poetry, *Jacklight* and *Baptism of Desire,* and of three novels, *Love Medicine, The Beet Queen* and *Tracks.*

Margaret Erhart has published a novel, *Unusual Company,* and has finished a second novel, *Augusta Cotton.* "Mothers, Daughters" was written in 1975. It is the first short story she ever wrote. Last year she began to study American Sign Language.

Ellen Gruber Garvey teaches creative writing and literature at the University of Pennsylvania, where she is completing a doctorate in English. Her work has appeared in numerous anthologies, including *Word of Mouth, Women's Glib, Speaking for Ourselves* and *Dreams in a Minor Key.* She was born in New York City in 1954 and presently lives in Brooklyn.

Vivian Gornick was born in New York City in 1935. She co-edited, along with Barbara Moran, *Woman in Sexist Society* in 1972. She is the author of *In Search of Ali Mahmoud: An American Woman in Egypt; Women in Science: Portraits from a World in Transition* and *Fierce Attachments: A Memoir.*

Gish Jen has had stories published in *The New Yorker, The Atlantic Monthly, Best American Short Stories* and *Home to Stay: Asian American Women's Fiction.* Her first novel, *Typical American,* will be published in 1991.

Linnea Johnson was born and raised on the East Side of Chicago. She has published a volume of poetry, *The Chicago Home,* and has had writing published in *Prairie Schooner, The Women's Review of Books, APR* and *Sinister Wisdom.* She teaches writing, literature and women's studies at a small college in Pennsylvania.

Barbara Kingsolver is the author of two novels, *The Bean Trees* and *Animal Dreams,* a collection of short stories, *Homeland,* and a non-fiction book entitled *Holding the Line: Women in the Great Arizona Mine Strike of 1983.*

Binnie Kirshenbaum is the author of the novel *Short Subject* and the short story collection *Married Life and Other True Adventures.* She was the recipient of a 1990-1991 Fellowship in Fiction from the New York Foundation for the Arts. She resides in New York City.

Marilyn Krysl has published five books of poetry and two books of stories. She teaches at the University of Colorado at Boulder. Her latest books are *What We Have to Live With* and *Midwife.* She has recently completed a novel, *Atomic Open House.*

Audre Lorde is a black lesbian feminist poet, prose writer and essayist. Her books include *Our Dead Behind Us, The Cancer Journals, Sister/Outsider, A Burst of Light* and *Zami: A New Spelling of My Name.*

Harriet Malinowitz was born in 1954 and lives in New York City. Her short fiction has appeared in numerous journals and anthologies including *Conditions, Sinister Wisdom, The Massachusetts Review, Nice Jewish Girls, Lesbian Love Stories,* and *My Father's Daughter.* Her first play, *Minus One,* was produced in June 1989 in New York City. She teaches writing at New York University, where she is also working on her doctorate in composition and rhetorical theory.

Christian McEwen was born in London in 1956 and grew up in Scotland. She is the editor of *Naming the Waves: Contemporary Lesbian Poetry* and the co-editor, along with Sue O'Sullivan, of *Out the Other Side: Contemporary Lesbian Writing.* She is currently working on a third anthology about feminism, race and class.

Valerie Miner is the author of *Blood Sisters, All Good Women, Winter's Edge, Movement, Murder in the English Department* and *Trespassing and Other Stories.* She earns her living by teaching and by traveling around the country giving readings and lectures.

Mary Jane Moffat was born in Seattle in 1932. She and Charlotte Painter co-edited *Revelations: Diaries of Women.* She is the editor of *In the Midst of Winter: Selections from the Literature of Mourning* and the author of *City of Roses: Stories from Girlhood* and *The Times of Our Lives: A Guide to Writing Autobiography and Memoir.*

Joyce Carol Oates was born in Lockport, New York in 1938.

She is a prolific author, well known for her many novels, poems, short stories, essays and plays. Her most recently published work includes *Because It is Bitter, and Because It is My Heart* and *I Lock My Door Upon Myself*.

Grace Paley was born in New York City in 1922. She is well known as an activist, writer and teacher. She is the author of three collections of short stories: *The Little Disturbances of Man, Enormous Changes at the Last Minute* and *Later the Same Day*.

Ntozake Shange, poet, novelist and playwright, is the author of *For Colored Girls Who Have Considered Suicide When the Rainbow is Enuf; Betsey Brown; Sassafrass, Cypress and Indigo; Ridin' the Moon in Texas: Word Paintings; A Daughter's Geography* and *See No Evil*.

Peggy Shinner lives in Chicago. In 1990 she helped to organize a retreat for AIDS caregivers in the Midwest. Her fiction has appeared in *Other Voices, Central Park, Sojourner, Naming the Daytime Moon* and *Another Chicago Magazine*.

Amy Tan was born in Oakland, California in 1952, two and a half years after her parents immigrated to the United States from China. Her first novel, *The Joy Luck Club*, was published in 1989. Her second novel, *The Kitchen God's Wife*, will be published in 1991.

S. L. Wisenberg was born in 1955 in Houston, Texas. She has been an amusement park cashier, English teacher in Nicaragua, au pair girl, and reporter for the *Miami Herald*. She has published in various genres in *The New Yorker, Calyx, Wigwag, The Progressive, Tikkun, Kenyon Review* and *Common Bonds: Stories By and About Modern Texas Women*.

Hilma Wolitzer was born in Brooklyn and now lives in Manhattan. She has published five novels for adults, four for children and several short stories. She has taught in the writing programs at the University of Iowa, Columbia University, N.Y.U. and at Bread Loaf.

Irene Zahava (editor) was born in the Bronx in 1951. She has owned and operated a feminist bookstore in upstate New York since 1981. She edits feminist titles and The WomanSleuth Mystery Series for The Crossing Press, and has compiled thirteen anthologies of women's writings, including *Through Other Eyes: Animal Stories by Women; Finding Courage; Word of Mouth* and *My Father's Daughter.*

*The Crossing Press
publishes a full selection of
feminist titles.
To receive our current catalog,
please call —Toll Free—800/777-1048.*